THE COUNT OF
SCOTLAND YARD

THE COUNT OF SCOTLAND YARD

THE CONTROVERSIAL LIFE AND CASES OF DCS HERBERT HANNAM

STEPHEN WADE

AMBERLEY

For Cathy

First published 2018

Amberley Publishing
The Hill, Stroud
Gloucestershire, GL5 4EP

www.amberley-books.com

Copyright © Stephen Wade, 2018

The right of Stephen Wade to be identified as
the Author of this work has been asserted in
accordance with the Copyrights, Designs and
Patents Act 1988.

ISBN 978 1 4456 8101 6 (paperback)
ISBN 978 1 4456 8102 3 (ebook)

British Library Cataloguing in Publication Data.
A catalogue record for this book is available
from the British Library.

Typesetting and Origination by Amberley Publishing
Printed in the UK.

CONTENTS

Preface   7

1 True Crime, Bert Hannam and the New Detectives   14

2 Enter Sergeant Hannam   36

3 A Confession from the Nick:
   The Walter Rowland Case, 1946   58

4 Probing Dollar Rackets, 1947   71

5 The Teddington Towpath Murders, 1953   83

6 Conspiracies, 1955   96

7 Did the Doctor Do It?, 1957   106

8 Called up North, 1957   159

9 The Man Himself and in Police History   168

10 A Summing-up   204

Appendix 1: 'Easing the Passing': Historical Perspectives   211

Appendix 2: Charles Hewett by David Hewett   217

Appendix 3: Corner Shop Murders   229

Appendix 4: Eastbourne   232

Notes and References   235

Bibliography and Sources   242

Acknowledgements   251

Index   253

PREFACE

Sometimes a writer's life borders on the obsessive: a theme or a subject work their way into the consciousness and the potential of a story never fades. That was the case with this book, and a little explanation is necessary to explain the genesis of Bert Hannam's biography. In an age when many biographies are of celebrities, this is insistently the opposite. It is a revisionary one, asking the reader to look back, and to look again.

At other times, one looks at the course of a life and nothing makes much sense: there may be no natural progression, no sense of a logical plan and no chronological certainty in the way the individual life progresses. From a writer's standpoint, such intractability does little more than remind one that an actual life does not follow logical templates, and that in most cases things happen according to circumstances. Thomas Hardy's interest in his characters' lives, for instance, often mixed the nature of their desires with the outward course of a life thrust upon them. Writing a biographical narrative can seem to be semi-fictional in this sense: research reveals certain facts and influences, but in the end, there is no pattern and one has to be forced on the plan of the book.

But the present work did not have that characteristic: it meant at first matching Bert Hannam's life to a string of major cases; then what kicked in was the occasional glimpse of the man himself. The latter came in such a piecemeal fashion that I left the account of the man and his life within his times until a later chapter, rather than keeping always to a chronology.

Sometimes, a writer has to work backwards to revisit the project that got away. Every writer, every historian is familiar with the tendency for new ideas for potential books to appear when a current book is progressing. This is what happened with *The Count of Scotland Yard*. At the time I first became aware of him, it was in the context of a regional work which involved little actual detail on the police personnel involved. But he stood out. He was from the era of the trilby hat, the gabardine raincoat and the man in the shadows, usually with a fag in the mouth. But he was not of that ilk at all. Everything pointed to his being something of a rebel, or perhaps simply a man who was a little eccentric, and that was fine, of course, as the last thing a biographer wants is the norm, the middle of the road.

It was not until I managed to obtain a copy of Bert Hannam's service record that reality stepped in. What is officially called the Central Record of Service contained the essence of Bert Hannam's life. There were the commendations and the key dates in his career.

There also was his signature: 'Herbert Wheeler Walter Hannam'. This was juxtaposed with the more mundane 'Robert Berry' and 'Charles Broom'. My suspicion that I had before me a remarkably individual character was beginning to be confirmed. The photographs backed up this first impression. Every image of him showed a man who appeared to have just walked out of a shop in Savile Row, with a fresh outfit on his sturdy, strong body.

He had been more than a bit player in a long saga of puzzling, indeed mesmerising murder cases; he was a reliable sidekick to others; he was also that rare breed, the many-sided talent who seemed to turn his hand to a wide spectrum of criminal cases and transgressions.

When I eventually came to communicate with the grandson of Bert and the son of Charles Hewett, Hannam's sergeant in his most famous case, there was the strange feeling that the public man, the one that the papers had been so keen to examine and exaggerate, was nowhere in evidence in his private life.

There is no greater challenge in life-writing than the enigmatic figure, the person who defies easy definition. My previous biographies had been of the artist Thomas Rowlandson, the operetta star George Grossmith, and the writer and explorer Harry de Windt. Grossmith and de Windt were public men with lots written about them. Rowlandson was more of the Hannam breed – well known to some but essentially reserved. Consequently, Hannam and his life proved to be a challenge to write, but one of a category I had previously encountered.

The work was retrospective, then, at the point at which I commenced research. Without some personal contact with family members or friends, my subject would have remained a man of mystery, even without the trilby and gabardine. It was unknown territory because I knew that there was no pre-existing biography, and I soon became aware that there may be only scant records. Still, the art of biography is to find the centre of the spine narrative of the individual life, and sometimes that is hidden in the personal, individuated experience of the subject, and sometimes it is only visible in the public life. When I wrote Rowlandson's life, it was with a similar awareness. Here was a man who existed almost entirely in his work. If he hadn't been a gambler and if there had not been two letters to go on, he would have remained a mystery.

Consequently, biography is, by its very nature, a dredging operation, down into the mud of time; our lives are embedded in the facts, experiences and footnotes allotted to us. In Hannam's case, the spine of the narrative was obviously in the major crimes he investigated; and yet, oddly, the chain of photographs over the years provided a slightly off-beat alternative story: a series of glimpses of a man which told another tale, at least hinted at one. That alternative story was there somewhere. In this dredging, what comes up into the light might be staggeringly new and unexpected or it may be mostly mundane and predictable, but the unknown factor in a life is what the writer always keeps in mind.

As a writer fascinated by past lives, I have always held to the dictum that the lives of people in the past are more often clouded by their own actions than by the greater world around them. Few keep journals or diaries. Most are not verbose when it comes to explaining their lives. In the end, the individual life is rarely valued by the person inside the skin: it is the writer or artist who insists on seeing the full picture. The writer longs for an exhaustive study, but the past offers only a rough sketch.

In the case of *The Count of Scotland Yard*, I learned more in the actual writing than I did in the early thinking and planning. In past projects, I had learned that there may be archives packed with material, but nothing of interest about the person as they really were. Life may generate paper, records and testimonies, but in the end, the biographer wants an interview, and that can't happen: it has to be imagined. My own interview with the Count would be about how he changed after each buffet from the storms of fate; again and again, life as a police officer threw at him something else to trip him up, make him look a fool, but he kept to his own beliefs and self-confidence and he did more than just survive.

What does a biographer do when much of the substance of his book comes from inference, spiced with a little guesswork? The answer is that he or she develops a structure relating to the great metanarrative of the world around the subject's life, and in the case of Bert Hannam, that metanarrative contained a world war, a Blitz on his home patch, and a society in which the moral compass had been cracked. Finding him inside this enfolding and dark realm of war and terror meant inferring his actions through the responses of others. Many people kept diaries during the war years; the Mass-Observation project, by which registered observers watched and reported on the daily lives of ordinary people, gave impressions of what it was like to live and work close up to the bombs, and the fear that Britain may lose and the population become servants of the Nazi regime. But for Hannam, this had to take second place to the urgency of the investigations in hand.

Criminal law, of course, has its own history too: the records of assizes, adversarial trials, appeals and committees are there to provide that strand in the narrative. But what of the police, the people caught in the crossfire on most occasions? What of the officers who turn up with their notebooks, ask questions, and have to correlate opinions and differences with what seem to be the facts? Who tells their story? Usually they do it themselves, and the stories are in transient form, as anyone who has tried to trace police ancestors will have discovered. Comments and facts go into occurrence books; sometimes there were records for burial societies or superannuation contributions, and we may learn about wounds suffered in the course of their duties. But normally we glimpse them through a few spoken words in the Old Bailey sessions papers or in press reports.

For all these reasons, *The Count of Scotland Yard* will be an attempt to find the man beneath the official reports, strangers' opinions and the memoirs of retired legal celebrities.

From the start, pictures seemed to tell more than words in print; my challenge is to find evidence about a man who ran from the limelight and preferred the shadows.

In spite of the above doubts and misgivings, however, the project has been most worthwhile and rewarding. There is a feeling that my attempt to secure a place for Bert Hannam alongside the other outstanding individuals of the police force of this country has been successful in drawing attention to a lamentable gap on the shelves where he should be. My argument is, in brief, that here was a man who worked tirelessly in every task he was given; his record shows regular switches from one specialist unit to another, peppering his CV with the abbreviations of the Yard's structure from the C numbers to X and Y. That record asserts his singular place in the modern history of British detectives: few can match his versatility. In a sense, my insistence on highlighting his abilities has been an effort to eclipse the superficial insistence of the media on wanting to tell the world that he was a smart, dapper, conceited individual. In place of that, I offer an account of someone much maligned, and certainly much misunderstood. At the start of my enquiries, he was much like Winston Churchill's definition of Russia, 'a riddle wrapped in a mystery inside an enigma', and I feel sure that Hannam would have been happy with that assessment.

Only with some accounts from his friends and colleagues did something a little more substantial come through.

Herbert Hannam began his police career in the Roaring Twenties and finished it on the eve of the Swinging Sixties. There was so much going on in that span of time that the decision had to be made to make this book a 'life and times'. His work was so close to so many nationally important events that the story cried out to be contextual, and so although the major cases take centre stage I have tried to bring in the wider picture. Interestingly, every aspect of his police life opens up something linking to contemporary themes and preoccupations in indirect ways, and I have found this in previous life-writing. But if we search, as historians, for that elusive thing called a *Zeitgeist* – a spirit of the age – then individual biographies help. The poet Gillian Clarke once said, when asked if books changed the world, that people read books, and books change people, so surely it's people who change the world.

Hannam never set out to change anything on a grand scale, but he wanted closure and justice. Sometimes they can be too much to ask for, but he never gave up. That has to be some kind of contribution to changing the world, even if only a little.

What more powerful image can there be of the nature of the public life than the image of an aged person speaking about his early life? Memorably, an instance of this came one day watching a documentary on the IRA. An old man, sitting in his comfortable armchair, spoke of killings and atrocities, calmly, factually and blandly. How could the viewer reconcile that old man with the young activist? They were from two worlds. That is how one feels when comparing Hannam the detective, surrounded by villains and involved in tough courtroom struggles, with the kind, quiet grandfather recalled by his grandson Iain.

I found that paradox to be a valuable help in this enterprise. It reinforced the view that the private and the public life are not necessarily mutually helpful in writing a life and may consequently be mutually exclusive. Wordsworth the young poet, exploring revolutionary France, is inevitably compared by biographers to the old man at home in the Lakes, complaining about railways.

Bert Hannam is at the heart of this book, but to assess him is as tough as any attempt to understand the past, like trying to grab a basketball with slippery hands. I hope that the reader will follow my efforts in this endeavour with interest.

TRUE CRIME, BERT HANNAM AND THE NEW DETECTIVES

Much of this biography is concerned with murder, the hunt for potential or probable killers and the struggle for justice to be applied. Consequently, before we commence with the life of our detective, he needs to be placed in the context of his genre and of his profession. Some reflections on the true crime genre are useful here, along with the place of detectives in it. After all, the detective came to cultural prominence in literature and cinema during Hannam's lifetime.

Being concerned with serious crime throws up serious matters, but popular literature inevitably stands in the way of historical truth and the search for authenticity. We need to place police biography in the context of a much more prominent theme. It relates to why police lives are constantly interesting.

'I love a good murder.' How many times have I heard that statement? In my youth, the somewhat questionable truth of the assertion was there to see every weekend, when my father opened his *News of the World* and turned with relish to savour a headline along the lines of 'Torso Found in Wood' or 'He Stabbed His Beloved Through the Heart'. Yes, there was that 'love' – but what a strange word to use alongside the heinous crime of taking a human life. The truth is, of course, that a murder story – even one about an actual case – is somehow transmuted from reality into a fascinating no-man's-land between fiction and fact when we see it in print.

Equally common is 'I love a good detective story', and in both cases – true crime books and sleuth novels – there is a need to look at the genre before embarking on a biographical enquiry. The statements are based on the apparent paradox that we find pleasure in reading about horrendous suffering and cruelty.

George Orwell understood this paradox. In his seminal essay on this subject, 'Decline of the English Murder', he suggested that the word 'pleasure' needed to be applied to this popular cultural phenomenon, and he even suggests a canon of template cases: 'Our great period in murder, our Elizabethan period so to speak, seems to have been between roughly 1850 and 1925, and the murderers whose reputation has stood the test of time are the following: Dr Palmer of Rugeley, Jack the Ripper, Neill Cream, Mrs Maybrick, Dr Crippen, Seddon, Joseph Smith, Armstrong, and Bywaters and Thompson.'

This reminds us that back in the early nineteenth century, Thomas de Quincey had enjoyed the wonderfully subtle humour of how murder stories were enjoyed, in his mock lecture on the 'fine art' of murder. Orwell almost takes that further by suggesting the canon of murders with ongoing reputations, as if we are in the trade of awarding status or league table positions to these killers.

There is no doubt that this fine art of murder steals the news headlines too. In his autobiographical work *Walden*, Henry David Thoreau wrote, 'After a night's sleep the news is as indispensable as the breakfast. "Pray tell me what has happened to any man anywhere on the globe" – and he reads it over his coffee and rolls, that a man has had his eyes gouged out this morning on the Wachito river...'

The activity of enjoying such tales needed a suitable adjective, and it was provided by a man who has been a presiding genius in my writing career for many years now. He is hardly a household name, but perhaps he should be, if a murder is such a nationally or even universally acknowledged media concern. The man I refer to is William Roughead (pronounced *rock-heed*).

William Roughead was born in Edinburgh in 1870. His father was a draper in Princes Street. But when his father, John Carfrae Roughead, drowned at sea off the Scilly Isles in 1887, the business was sold. William began his studies at Edinburgh University, taking up law, but did not complete his degree programme. He had been articled to a law firm in George Street, and, having a comfortable income from the sale of his father's business, had no pressing need to follow the normal route into a professional career. William had developed an interest in dramatic criminal trials, and this became his primary concern, forming the basis of his future success in writing. Despite the aborted course of his legal studies, Roughead entered the law by another route: he became a writer to the signet. The word 'writer' here is a Scottish term for 'lawyer', and the post was linked to the status of the private seal of Scottish kings, and so Roughead was basically a solicitor, his name appearing in the official Scottish Law List. From his time as a student through to the year 1949, three years before his death, he was there in the Edinburgh High Court whenever there was a trial for murder.

Roughead began his writing life as a poet and editor, but his entrance into the 'criminous' world as an author was from the springboard provided by the company that has been forever linked with high-quality and scholarly publishing of crime records: Hodge. To the *aficionado* of crime and courtroom analysis, the *Notable Trials* series is a template of excellence. Hodge was a friend of Roughead's and together they started *Notable Scottish Trials* with a volume on Dr Edward Pritchard, a Glasgow doctor who poisoned his wife and his mother-in-law. Roughead's role was to be editor of the volume, a book that would have to cover the process of the trial in detail. It set the standard for what was to follow, such was Roughead's expertise and depth of knowledge of the trajectory of a high-profile trial. He also had the research skills to back up the local knowledge.

In my library of old volumes on crime and law, I have a special collection of books by this man – a figure widely regarded as the one who first tried to make true crime a branch of literature, rather than a subsection trapped in the 'Penny Dreadful' genre in popular Victorian publishing. Roughead wrote an essay called 'The Enjoyment of Murder', which sums up this dubious and puzzling pleasure, and in this he makes it clear that he is not a criminologist: 'All I claim to do is to tell a tale of crime well and truly; to supply the psychologically minded with reliable grist for their recondite mills; and to give, if possible, the gentle reader as much pleasure in the perusal as I found in the writing.' That would be my apologia also for my writings in the criminous vein.

There we have the word then: *criminous*. The adjective aspires to define, though loosely, that intrigue we have with the narrative of horrendous or at least puzzling criminal transgression. This encompasses the professional Ripperologists as well as those who buy and enjoy the red-and-black crime magazines every month, but it also includes the higher end of the spectrum: the works in which true crime is a genre bordering on multi-layered biography, social history and even amateur psychology. In recent years, this end of the spectrum in the genre is perhaps exemplified by Kate Summerscale's *The Suspicions of Mr Whicher* (2008). I attempted this kind of project in *The Girl Who Lived on Air* in 2014, in which I revisited arguably the most famous crime story in Victorian Wales, involving Sarah Jacob, the so-called Welsh Fasting Girl. In my efforts I discovered that, for the amateur sleuth, this demanded intense research into both the legal definition of manslaughter in 1869 and the workings of the Welsh jury. Roughead's notion of what was criminous related as much to the world of detectives as to that of criminals. In his time, he studied the law and its workers alongside the villains who hanged.

Later, the world of true crime was to come through as my principal concern, something that fired the imagination. This is because the criminous narrative invariably mixed with transgression in the moral sphere of human society. Attempting to define the attraction of true crime literature means facing the complex nature of shifting moral structures. What was a heinous crime in 1790 may now be nothing more than a petty misdemeanour. This maintains the fascination in the true crime genre.

What is the heart of the matter, then, when we speak or write of 'true crime' and its 'criminous' interest? The answer surely lies in some matter to be drawn from Bruce Robinson's massive tome, *They All Love Jack*. This is the result of a fifteen-year study of the Ripper and the social, cultural, forensic and justicial world around the Whitechapel murders. Robinson expended immense time and energy demonstrating that, with enough effort, a considerable amount of circumstantial detail may be accrued if one is determined to create a new suspect for Jack. Mr Justice Hawkins, later Lord Bramwell, would no doubt have been keen to convict Mr Michael Maybrick had he appeared before him in court, because the noble judge gave much credence to the circumstantial. Sadly, though, there is a mass of information but very little actual evidence gathered in the book.

The book is a compelling, richly layered read, and I had to read it almost without a break over four days. Bruce Robinson did a magnificent job, but unfortunately the book will sit alongside its partners in that ever-growing library of suspect studies. But my point is that it is in the generating of counter-narratives that we readers and writers of the genre find our delight. In *Murder in Mind* I use my own very favourite case study in murder: the tale of alleged murderess Louie Calvert of Leeds, who was hanged in Strangeways in 1926 for the murder of Lily Waterhouse. I investigated the case with a little of that zeal Bruce Robinson has in abundance; I have the witness statements, the police correspondence, the fingerprints, the documentation regarding the trial, and everything else – except a picture of tiny, brown-haired Louie. I also have my own theory, and I have relished putting that on paper. The appeal of the criminous was that I was impelled by a desire to examine justice and help others look again at a case which history has, I feel, misrepresented.

There is also another dimension of criminous activity which must be examined – and celebrated. This is the preoccupation with the need to empathise with (as well as to understand) those involved in horrible crimes. I first became aware of just how deeply this is embedded when I researched my book *Conan Doyle and the Crimes Club*. This is about the beginnings of the Crimes Club, which still exists today, and this club illustrates the nature of the 'criminous' as it borders on various areas of expertise. It began as a mix of amateurs and professionals, but at its heart it was Roughead's domain shifted into affable, sociable literary and legal recreation. It was wining and dining, with talks and debate.

The Crimes Club was the first outfit into amateur detection. The new detective had just arrived; fingerprints had come on to the scene, and there was a need for more professionalism in detective work, with better forensics to back it up. The club members represented a fair proportion of the literary and legal elite of their generation: they had excelled in the professional worlds of writing, commerce, litigation and highbrow journalism; they loved to meet in convivial and relaxed surroundings, and they enjoyed parading their conversational talents in front of gaggles of like-minded men, perhaps at ease with brandy and a cigar, or sometimes giving a learned and entertaining talk about a topic of general interest. Peter Costello, in his book *Conan Doyle: Detective*, wrote that 'the members were … so many students of contemporary crime. But they kept their affairs secret, so that even today … little has been divulged about them. The club still exists and remains, as ever, exclusively secret.'

They were at first named 'Our Society' but later became the Crimes Club. They first assembled at the Great Central Hotel in London on 17 July, 1904, after being discussed informally at the home of the son of the great actor Sir Henry Irving, Harry Brodribb Irving, the year before. This was followed by a dinner at the Carlton Club in December 1903, and from that it is certain that the more formal conditions and guidelines for activities were formed. Although members wanted the club to remain easy and chummy, with chats about fascinating criminal memorabilia or talks on infamous cases by professional members who were in the legal profession, word got around, and others wanted to join in.

They were an assortment of mainly university men, many from Oxford, where they had learned the importance of networking, although back then the word used for that was simply *society*. They had all acquired the gentlemanly accomplishments expected of men of letters who wanted to stay in favour among their peers in the publishing world of the time. Most of them could be called, in the parlance of the twenty-first century, movers and shakers. But more important was the fact that they had a common interest and saw the benefits of sharing knowledge and experience.

The meetings soon attracted all kinds of members, and in 1909, one of the original members, Ingleby Oddie, a coroner, resigned; he was miffed at the new identity of the club – something more streamlined and academic than first conceived. The other founding members were largely from the ranks of literary celebrity and aristocracy: Sir Arthur Conan Doyle, Churton Collins, James Beresford Atlay, Lord Albert Edward Godolphin Osborne, George R. Sims, Max Pemberton, Fletcher Robinson, Harry Irving, C. A. (Lord) Pearson and A. E. W. Mason. Among the less well-known were Arthur Lambton and a medical man from Norwich, Dr Herbert Crosse.

Their great delight was in being close to the people and cases they wrote about. Collins, for instance, knew the Tichborne Claimant very well, and visited him in prison and later in his lodgings. As a club, they were taken on a walk around the Ripper haunts. It became evident to me as I first read about them that the crime scene is the very foundation of criminous writing, and it is a vitally important element in the empathic motivation on the part of readers and writers.

These men were not professionals like Bert Hannam. But what the Crimes Club did foreshadow was the new world of crime detection and study that came along in the 1930s with the Trenchard reforms, the expansion of police training and the increasingly high-level work done at Peel House, up to and throughout the war years, in producing high-quality men and women for the police forces of the land. By the 1920s, when Hannam joined the Metropolitan Police, the detective was fashionable, cool and sexy. Readers knew that top detectives not only solved murders but were often involved in espionage as well, and in protecting the vulnerable at the same time as they were morally above suspicion. The new approaches to detective training in the 1930s were extremely thorough. The volumes produced after a committee report into the subject break down every identified skill in detective work conceivable at the time. It is plain to see that the almost ninety years since the formation of the first proper detective force had been a period in which successive waves of new crimes produced reactive steps in the ranks of the top brass as they tried to combat the new threats to social order. Within that ninety years, there had emerged Fenian terrorism, anarchy from Russian émigrés after pogroms in their homelands, espionage in the early years of the twentieth century, and then the essential establishment of specialist bureaus within the Yard as forensics advanced.

Yet the detectives themselves moved, and still move, in a world somewhere between fact and fiction, as far as the public is concerned. Today, the proliferation of detective dramas forces on the general reader and viewer the notion that the sleuth is on the side of good in a fallen world. Bert Hannam joined the ranks of these good men in the 'mean streets' that Raymond Chandler's Philip Marlowe walked. Yet he was soon to find, through the 1940s and 1950s, that there were far more difficult enemies in the detective's path than gangs or psychopaths. There was politics, and the invisible workings of political power, filtering through all levels of society. In his brief was the need to – somehow – deal with this.

Then there is the advance of science. Since 1984 and the first application of DNA in a murder case, with all its attendant difficulties for the court process, the detective has had to be *au fait* with the forensics around him in procedure and in investigation. Hannam retired before all that, but his specific challenge was to function and to succeed in the raw and heartless world of post-war tough luck and dire necessity. When he began his career, though, in 1927, it was at a time when forensics was an exciting subject, in the hands of the great Bernard Spilsbury, whose charismatic personality attracted the press at every trial he was involved in. Hannam would have had to gain a sound basic knowledge of forensic work during his training at Peel House just as war loomed. The war was to bring detectives much closer to scene of crime work when murders occurred in the ruins of the Blitz, notably through the efforts of the Blackout Ripper, Gordon Cummins, who committed several murders around London in 1942 when Hannam was at work nearby.

In a sense, the discipline of criminology effaces and perhaps destroys true crime, as the latter, in the canonical cases Orwell isolates and perhaps in all celebrated cases, relies for its impact on a certain degree of wonder. The criminous wants the human being to be a mystery wrapped in an enigma. At the core of true crime narrative, in its primitive form, it thrives on the investigation conducted by fallible, though determined people with no DNA analysis, no forensic entomology, in their armoury; the motivation for a crime needs to be something enigmatic, something facing the reader like a coded challenge. But at the same time, Aristotle's dictum that we go to experience tragedy for reasons of 'pity and fear' is still there. He located the interest in the fact that the tragic hero is 'of us but not like us'. That is, we recognise the murderous illogicality of Othello's knife being plunged into Desdemona's breast as being something our species might be capable of, but we preserve the belief in our rationality and our defences against madness and homicidal mania, taking comfort in the assurance that we will always see such behaviour as evil or insane.

Hannam lived and worked in the milieu of increasingly complex murders; this was so because psychology and its applications in criminal behaviour brought new challenges. He was working before the emergence of so much that we now encounter in criminal investigations, such as mapping, profiling and internet communications. But this places his work and cases interestingly more in the world of the popular crime magazines than in textbooks, and that has its special and irresistible appeal. More than anything else back then, reliance was on fingerprint traces.

As time has sped on and supplied true crime narratives which offer far more complexity than Orwell's classic template of cases, abnormal psychology has added a number of dimensions to transgression which previously were outside enquiry. The traditional theory of the bourgeois illusion of rationality, in which the baddie will be punished and the victim will have justice and his fellow citizens will be protected, has had to be challenged – but not dismissed. It still persists as an important part of the criminous impulse we have in the genre, but if it is to be prolonged, the traditional narrative still has to be there at the core of the story. Personally, as a writer, my basis of thought in researching murder is always related to Shakespeare's line about King Lear: 'He hath ever but slenderly known himself.' Everywhere we turn we may see the crime story that hinges totally on that insight. Perhaps the clearest instance in modern times of that is in the case of Neville Heath, who may or may not have been truly aware of his terrible duality. The media 'monster' often turns out to be someone who but slenderly knows himself, with catastrophic consequences.

In researching cases from the years of hanging, and in particular murders before the 1861 Offences Against the Persons Act, when capital crimes were radically reduced in number, I have often been struck by the classic narrative:

Situation and conflict – murder – chase – trial – retribution

The last word in this sequence is where the popular cultural ingredient for Roughead and the classic writers lies most potently: the destination of the culprit. In the most horrendously retributive years of the Georgians and early Victorians, the potential destinations were noose, prison, madhouse or pardon/acquittal/commutation. Again, with Aristotle in mind, and his insistence that in our engagement with any story, a part of us is – from the very beginning – anticipating closure, the shadow of the noose or the prison-house in the years when over 200 capital offences were on the statute books added the most compelling element in the tale. Bert Hannam was working in these days of the noose, and that hard fact coloured so much of a murder investigation, as may clearly be seen in the famous Bodkin Adams case, and equally urgently in the Balchin murder.

Arguably, Thomas de Quincey wrote the definitive account of our tendency to make real crime into something akin to art in his essay with the title 'On Murder Considered as one of the Fine Arts'. I encourage anyone not familiar with that *tour de force* to read it and revel in its fun and pastiche. But he was writing long before the whole business of literature moved to the sophisticated and rarefied world beyond the *Newgate Calendar* and any number of 'pulp fiction' and 'Horrible murder' publications. What he really understood, however, was that there is a peculiarly British flavour to that Sunday afternoon time with the paper and the gruesome domestic slaughter it details.

Is there a conclusion to this line of thought about what the criminous is and why it permeates the true crime genre so deeply? If there is, then it has to have something to do with our confrontation with the dark stranger inside us, the bad *daemon*, the Mr Hyde, the one that psychology tries to argue away with abstraction and analysis. It has everything to do with the unsettling realisation that, if he or she or it really does lie somewhere within us – even as a minute sequence in our DNA composition – then the last thing we want is for him or her or it to remain a stranger. We want to face that being; we might instantly look away if the perception does actually disturb us, but we *so* want to look. In the life and work of 'The Count of Scotland

Yard' we have a perfect template of that fascinating and somehow inscrutable figure, the charismatic lawman. He might have been dapper and seemingly 'posh', but he was not so far from Wyatt Earp – though his confrontations were in court rather than in any OK Corral.

A policeman's lot, as every Gilbert and Sullivan fan will tell us, 'is not a happy one'. When the professional police officer was first created by Sir Robert Peel's Act of 1829, the public thought that military law would grab hold of their lives and freedom would come to an end. For many decades, the life of a police officer, and especially of a detective after they first appeared in 1842, was tough in every department, and by the time that Herbert Hannam joined the Metropolitan Police in the 1920s, the lawmen had weathered many a storm concerning their profession and its status and esteem. But it was an exciting time to sign up to serve in the noble uniform of the British police force. A revolution in training and organisation was happening.

There is also the matter of biographies of people within the criminal justice system in general. First, why write the life of a police detective? The answer is obvious when it comes to the detectives who were involved in such cases as the Yorkshire Ripper or the Krays. The public has a steady readership with an interest in killers, and so there will always be room for such biographies. The same applies with lawyers; over the late twentieth century, a number of barristers and judges followed on from such celebrities as Travers Humphries and Lord Birkenhead in the first decades of that century. But when it comes to the interest motivating most of these, the discussion usually moves into such topics as 'character' and 'personality'. Well, there has to be some agreement about the importance of the subject of a biography being intrinsically interesting, but also the professional career has to have its special appeal.

I am able to claim both aspects of biographical interest in this work, and this is because my subject had the good fortune to be a man with special and particular skills; he was a man of his time, but in some principal respects he was a man out of his time as well. That is to say, he coped admirably with the demands of contemporary policing and procedure, but his personal qualities gave him another dimension. This irritated some and charmed others. Such is the appeal of a subject to a biographer.

There are lives lived in service to the public, and they consist of little more than that. Some people appear to want no more than a superficial public self; but others cultivate an extraordinary persona and project that into the public image of themselves. Hannam was the latter, and for a biographer, that projection of the 'Count' is as much a problem as it is a gift.

There is no doubt that Bert Hannam was an extraordinary man, and an equally extraordinary detective, but he is not strikingly unusual in the course of his career. Looked at in the context of many of his peers, his experiences were as varied as those of many other men, and his results comparable to the average. But his life can nevertheless be seen as strikingly dramatic and full of incident. Where his life is truly compelling for the biographer, and consequently for the reader, is in one massive, dominating event: the story of John Bodkin Adams, the Eastbourne doctor who has overshadowed almost everything else in Hannam's life, and whose controversial status in the annals of modern criminal trials is singularly dramatic. This case is as baffling as it is complex. With this in mind, some prefatory remarks are needed, one feels, to stress for the reader the oppositional forces at work which have gathered around the Adams case of 1957.

That trial is now well over half a century old, but it filled the national papers for many weeks and spawned books and articles which tend to be placed at direct opposites. At the very heart of these oppositions stands Hannam himself, a key player in the trial. What had perpetuated interest in the Adams case, almost as much as the doctor himself, was the partisan position of Percy Hoskins, crime editor of *The Daily Express*, favourite of Lord Beaverbrook and a very hearty companion to the doctor himself. He took pride in his press photographs, and there was something in him that loved the limelight. He allowed pictures of himself relaxing with Adams to be included in his book, *Two Men Were Acquitted*, without any apparent sense that such a connection would demolish any notion the reader might have of his impartiality regarding Hannam.

That fact, regardless of any other elements in this biography, would be enough to provoke a writer to assemble a counter-argument to the standard reading of the Adams case. Therefore, shamelessly, in the chapter on the Adams case there is a defence of Hannam. A biographer does not have to take sides; he or she may relish the pleasures of disinterest. There is no necessity to argue a case for matters to be revised, but there is, in this instance, a need to provide something to explain Hannam's work and attitudes, because he never wrote a memoir.

Some omissions have been necessary. I would have liked to include more information on currency regulation or Hannam's co-operation with the FBI. It seemed, when the book was conceived, to make more sense to provide the reader with the whole narrative of the major trials and investigations which have stuck to Bert Hannam's name and reputation. But at least something is known about the financial investigations, albeit little.

Hannam has been badly served in some quarters of the media, and at times during the research for this book there has been a lament that he never had a chance to speak fully. It appears that he never felt the need to do so – and this is the man whom Percy Hoskins considered to be a media darling. The fact is that Hannam could never resist a challenge. One of the classic works on the character of Dr Samuel Johnson is called *Johnson Agonistes*, the term indicating one who enjoys participating in the cut and thrust of human interchange of ideas and opinions. Beneath his professional adherence to due process and proper procedure, one feels that Hannam was *Bert Agonistes*.

He was also part of a dynasty. His son and grandson became police officers, and as I was preparing this book I spoke to former detective Stuart Gibbon, who graduated from the Police College in 1981. He had been in Trenchard House, the famous police hostel in London. In his special commemorative brochure there was a portrait of Kenneth Hannam, Bert's son. The dynasty was in safe hands, and when a letter from Kenneth to Percy Hoskins came into my hands, I deduced from Kenneth's words and writing style something of his father: civilized, restrained, balanced and gentlemanly while at the same time being incisive and to the point. It was not difficult to find echoes of some of those copious reports his father had written in his dogged pursuit of facts and of truth.

This persistence was professional practice, never driven by any kind of malign intention to get even or to score a point. The sleuth has to be fair to all parties, and most of all to the truth as he sees it from evidence gathered. Writing this biography has convinced the present writer that everyone needs someone to speak in their defence – particularly the silent dead, whose names gather respect and reverence.

When a notably unusual and demanding case comes along in the course of police history, the top brass look around for the right man or woman for the task ahead; Hannam was fortunate in that he gathered the kind of experience, in the early phase of his police career, that qualified him for dealing with a specific customer: the more wealthy, high-status and professional criminal or potential criminal. That is not to say that he never worked on the seedier side of violent crime; the Towpath case and the Ballast Hole killing demonstrate that. But his mind was finely tuned towards more intellectual habits, and he could take a distant, philosophical stance on matters. His very appearance would have suggested to a passer-by that here was a man who was perhaps a member of a Piccadilly club and who enjoyed fine dining and good company. Anything that might mark a man as being different from the norm can potentially have a negative effect on reputation or esteem.

After a thorough reading of the literature around the Towpath and Bodkin Adams cases, I have come to see that a biographer sometimes feels compelled to take sides. This is because, as the reader will see, Hannam himself was as often 'in the dock' and under scrutiny as much as the accused themselves in his cases. By 'take sides' the implication is that Hannam has been much assailed by those who resented his methods; that was usually because his fervour and resolve to be meticulous and dogged in his pursuit of the truth made enemies. Overall, he has been much maligned, and perhaps the reason that he wrote no memoir is linked to a feeling that he was so much the subject of press attention that he had had quite enough of the limelight, thank you.

This is not to say that my version of events will not consider opposing viewpoints with impartiality; on the contrary, to write a life is to weigh up and consider all sides. But the fact is that every major book-length publication on the major cases in Hannam's life has contained criticisms which spring from his rigorous approach to investigation. Surely that is what detectives do: they detect. That entails investigating sources and actions in order to find a truth, a factual basis on which to work.

I unashamedly offer the case for the defence – of Bert Hannam. But that is not to say that the case for the prosecution, to carry on the metaphor, will be discounted. The police officer is caught in the crossfire, in a sense, in an uneasy position in the dynamics of the criminal justice system. His or her actions in a criminal trial may often be more of a challenge than the actions in an investigation. In Hannam's case, it was his fate to be in the headlights when it came to high-profile murder trials.

Delving into his presence in these cases has not been plain sailing, except in the Whiteway and the Bodkin Adams case. In most others, he was always an effective and valued element in the work done, but tended to be one of a team, often doing plenty of footwork and shaping the material at the base of investigations.

Paradoxically, it is in the interstices of the documentation of some police work where he appears, even in the early phase of his career, and so it has been necessary to read between the lines. When he retired, aged fifty, he had done thirty-one years of service, and left with an exemplary certificate of conduct.

This has to be one of those biographies, then, which is mostly concerned with the main professional work, but from his exit from the force in 1958 to his death in 1983 there were many years which have, unfortunately, run together with little information. But he did more work after he left the police, and his lack of any urge to document the detective work indicates a need to brush it off and be someone else, live a totally different life. He did that. Sometimes the professional life and its span tends to offer more than enough excitement. A murder investigation tends to occupy the mind of the detective and it plagues him like flies around a horse. He must have been glad to shake this off.

What about the world of the Yard detective which young Hannam stepped into in the mid-1930s? Detectives were definitely sensationalised – and always newsworthy.

Crazy stories of 'detectives' proliferated as the popular media made them glamorous. Magazines such as *Union Jack* and the *Sexton Blake Library* (the latter started in 1915) had led to such innovations as 'The Dog Detective', and the blurb typified the appeal of the detective for readers: 'A Sexton Blake story means something really first class in the way of detective fiction. And you can get one every week! Stories that get you worked up with excitement, stories in which baffling mystery, non-stop action, brilliant detection and thrills are welded into one masterly whole...' The impact of such tales is shown in the case of 'sham detective' William Martin, who was arrested for the theft of thirty-two sides of bacon. He had carried out the theft by approaching a young boy who was in charge of the vanload of bacon, saying he was a detective and showing a badge. The boy said, 'I have seen detectives on the films wearing badges, so I believed him.'

Private detectives on divorce cases and Scotland Yard men involved in special duties alike were bringing to light a whole tranche of new issues related to the morality of detective work. A detective had to encroach on personal liberties in the course of his or her work; investigative actions would sometimes flirt with crossing the line into criminality, at least as far as the letter of the law would have it in a criminal law court.

This whole area of detective work became apparent during the First World War, when 'spy mania' meant that Vernon Kell and his new MI5 were intercepting letters; Kell worked with the Yard, and Yard men would learn to act as agents with a more military purpose. These difficulties became more widely understood with the Janvier case of 1917, which went to the Court of Appeal in 1919. Henriette Janvier had come from Paris to London in 1908 to learn English, sent there by her employers. During the First World War she met a German called Neumann. When her lodging house was almost empty one day in 1917, two agents (described as 'private enquiry agents') arrived and told Henriette that another lodger called March was corresponding with a spy and requested to access his post. On their first appearance, however, one of the agents had said, 'I am a Detective Inspector from Scotland Yard and represent the military authorities, and you are the woman we want, as you have been corresponding with a German spy.' Janvier fell ill from shock at this, and subsequently raised an action against the men for damages.

The truth was either that the two men really were Yard officers doing the usual thing and intercepting suspect mail, or that they were indeed private agents. If the latter, then they would have had no palpable reason for being on such a detail and to act as aggressively as they did. The incident illustrates the extent to which the presence of a Scotland Yard detective instilled awe and fear into private citizens. Of course, the Henriette affair was in a time of war, but in effect the detectives were asking the girl to co-operate in an enquiry – and one that breached civil rights – without prior arrangement. Moreover, they did that after first terrifying her.

The other major development before the end of the Second World War was the refinement of records. That incorporates the Criminal Records Office (CRO), which developed from the Habitual Criminals Register and has existed since 1871, together with the General Registry, within the Records Management Branch (QPP3). Records from Special Branch were separated from the main stock in 1946. The General Registry covers virtually everything from accidents to transport; two additional indices are maintained, these being the Names Index and Tag Index. The second one deals with matters by subject areas.

The crime correspondent of *The Daily Telegraph*, Stanley Firmin, writing in 1953, gave a brilliant description of the records at a time when the outstanding detective Robert Lee was working in the CRO. Firmin wrote that housed in the Criminal Records Office was the world's most complete collection of facts about individual criminals. That collection, built up over long years, consisted of much more than many hundreds of thousands of fingerprints; it had long embraced the filing away of all kinds of personal data about countless crooks throughout Britain.

Lee went to work in Records, and his time there illustrates the benefits of persistent use of information and sifting of data; Firmin explained that Lee built up an image of the suspect from details on squares of cardboard. He also came up with new ways of filing the records. His thesis for the innovations was that detailed knowledge constructed a personal profile, and that in turn became something that could be extended into predictive thinking – anticipating crimes. The evidence for this is in a case in which Lee and Records teamed up with the Ghost Squad, a special cadre of men and women which lasted from 1945 to 1949, devised as a network of officers working underground, taking on close observation of suspects. It was a concept familiar to espionage masters, of course. It was conceived by Percy Worth and developed by Commissioner Sir Ronald Howe. There is no doubt that the Ghost Squad was effective: in those few years their activities brought about 769 arrests and the recovery of over £200,000 worth of goods.

There is some doubt, but it does appear that Ghost Squad members were sometimes bribed and corrupted, and that happened in Lee's famous case, the dogged pursuit of a gang of robbers, with C. S. William Chapman of the Flying Squad (nicknamed the Terrier because of his determined and patient pursuit of suspects) leading the chase. Lee studied a long list of burglaries and looked for a pattern; he found one. The lead was a broken key in a safe, which turned out to be a unique key made by just one firm. Chapman than set about using the Ghost Squad to watch every employee of the firm, as it seemed certain that an employee was in the burglary ring. The observations lasted a very long time and there was a breakthrough, but in spite of Lee's excellent work there appears to have been some corruption of officers. In the end, the spy in the Yard was outwitted by Lee, who devised the clever plan of placing false duty rotas in the books so that the spy could not have accurate information to pass on to the crooks. The spy was never found, but the mastermind of the criminals, Santro the safe-breaker, was eventually caught, along with most (but not all) of the gang.

By the end of the Second World War, then, detectives were proliferating in all areas of life, but Scotland Yard and the CID were merging into a massive, many-sided organisation, with ever-increasing numbers of specialists and departments. Hannam, like many of his colleagues, was to experience life in several departments.

2

ENTER SERGEANT HANNAM

Top detectives are often quiet men. An inner dialogue dominates, and that is always going to be an unknown quantity for a biographer. Even some of the most renowned detectives, such as Jonathan Whicher, whom Dickens knew, along with his peers in the first wave of detectives in London, sat in anonymity until someone came along to shine a torch into the darkness where their personalities lay. The Jack the Ripper phenomenon – now an industry – brought to light such men as detectives Thomas Arnold, Walter Dew and others involved in the hunt for the killer, but even those people are far from household names. It is a profession loitering in the shadows; most of the work involved is patient, repetitive enquiry and logging of information.

If a search is done for the top detectives of the post-war years, for many there will be memoirs in print. They may not all be the kind of cops who figured in the black-and-white crime movies of the fifties involving Fabian of the Yard, but many did have some kind of status as comic-book heroes, and their lives were bursting with action and drama. However, there were some in these ranks who had no desire to leave their stories in print. Your name on the spine of a book is a kind of memento, and it is the fruit of a worthy enterprise, but there are many sleuths who see such tomes as no more than fragments of a gravestone and they see no point in them. Such a man was Herbert Hannam. He was a major player in several prominent and controversial murder cases, but he saw no point in recording this for the world. The present volume takes this up, as a tribute to the man, and as testimony to a respected and revered detective in arguably the best police force in the world.

Hannam did become known with that suffix 'of the Yard', and in his case it was 'the Count of Scotland Yard' because he was a smart, well-dressed man, a copper who cared about how he looked and acted; he cared about style. Long before there was any talk of being 'branded' in one's profession, he made such an identity. Pictures of him show a man who walked tall and proud; he had a swagger. Images often make it clear that he walked ahead of his junior officers. Often in his wake is Detective Sergeant Hewitt. One typical shot shows them walking in Eastbourne during the Adams trial; Hannam strides on ahead, turning slightly, with the hint of a smile on his face, and behind there is Hewitt, with a broad smile. They are surely sharing a joke.

Such a picture says so much about Bert Hannam. It confirms the view that he was popular and something of a 'character', of course, but it also shows clearly that he was not snooty and distant when with colleagues. There was no Malvolio in him. His typical attire when on duty was a bowler hat, smart dark suit, white shirt and a tie, black shoes shiny as a mirror, and skin gloves. Not for him the ragged, dishevelled 'Sweeney' look. The press attention to all this is so widespread, and so often repeated, that it seems as though the image was cultivated, in order to be 'the Count' of his nickname – to reinforce his uniqueness.

Why write the life of such a man? The answer is very clear. He was not simply a flamboyant personality in the grey, bland fifties; he was a detective with charisma, and he was often the man sent for when, in a tough investigation, someone had to be 'cracked' or an obstruction to progress removed.

As the subject of chapter six will show, Hannam was not confined to London in his activities. As in the Emily Pye murder, he was called north with his crack team, his instincts for good policing and his flair for effective organisation. His role in the case reads like that of a troubleshooter, brought in from the great metropolis, just as the Bow Street Runners often were back in the Regency years. The press reports sometimes made him seem like a miracle worker, and that was going much too far; the truth is that it was his presence, his air of confidence and assurance which created a mood of optimism. It is easy to imagine the whispers that *Hannam is on the case.*

In the fifties, such a colourful character was sorely needed. It was a grey time – in both landscape and in atmosphere. The deprivations of the war lingered on, with rationing imposed until 1953. The arduous and lengthy rebuilding after the Blitz was ongoing as Hannam was at work across the land. There was also the first inkling of teenage rebellion and unrest in the appearance of the Teddy Boys, with their loud versions of Edwardian clothing, their knives and bike chains, and their gang mentality. Their parents had fought a desperate war, of course, but they sensed that new times were coming, and that these would be different. But they were not the only transgressors in Hannam's world of post-war chaos; weapons retained after war service provided instruments of fear for corner-shop robberies and muggings, and there was a gangland network, much of it linked to London, where Hannam first learned his police work.

When Bert Hannam came into the middle phase of his career, in the fag-end of the war, there was a climate of intense dissent and conflict in terms of law and order. Police reforms just before 1939 had meant a certain streamlining of the force structures, but the Blitz and the collapse of standard morality had brought with it a new questioning of how the police should work, and in particular how the detective personnel should figure in a world in which violent crime was thriving and in which black market transgressions were rife.

In January 1947 announcements were made by the press concerning the expansion of the Metropolitan Police detective force; a crime wave was perceived and lamented generally, and in response, the papers reassured the public, the Home Secretary and the Commissioner of the Met, Sir Harold Scott, convened to discuss the issue. The result was that the manpower of the Met was to be increased to over 20,000. Some 200 new detectives were to be recruited, some of them pulled from those already serving their probationary periods.

Detectives were certainly busy in all quarters in these years; shots were fired at officers, most notably in St Johns Wood when two armed robbers went to work depriving the wealthy of their jewels; detectives even conducted raids on offices of the Fourth International (a Trotskyist faction) in Paddington in April 1944. On top of this there was the recurrent buzzword, 'corruption', which the press loved to throw around from time to time. In early 1944, for instance, two detectives were in court at the Old Bailey for taking bribes from the manager of the Adam and Eve in Homerton High Street. They were discharged.

This was the atmosphere in which young Bert Hannam learnt his trade; the old saying 'may you live in interesting times' may suggest action and suspense, but it also brings with it the storm and stress of a post-war world trying to adjust to accelerated change and threats to public order and safety in all corners of the land.

For most top detectives who figured in the major crimes of history, it is often one investigation that defines them. This is exemplified by the life of Jack Slipper, who will always be remembered as the officer who brought the Great Train Robbers to justice. But even in this instance, there was failure as well as determination. The obituaries in August 2005 pointed out that Slipper chased Ronnie Biggs to Brazil but came back empty-handed. Hannam was just as persistent when on the trail of a rogue, and had just as much frustration in the case of his most high-profile opponent, Dr Bodkin Adams. Yet his success rate was impressive, and it is a compliment to his reputation and professionalism that he was the man called in to carry out demanding and complex investigations throughout the fifties.

*

Herbert Wheeler Walter Hannam was born in Paddington on 29 July 1908, a child of that golden age of which historians write; pre-First World War, when Edward VII in his playboy lifestyle conveyed to his nation the necessity of fun, leisure and recreation. Before joining the Metropolitan Police in December 1927 Hannam was a pastry cook, and his four years of absorbing the art of baking tell us a great deal about the man. The artist Chaim Soutine painted a famous portrait of a pastry cook in 1922, and the image he gives us is of a puny, undersized boy swaddled in the white garb of the trade; his face expresses boredom and stoicism and his hands clutch a red cloth, as if he has paused between his onerous tasks. The life of a person in the baking profession was hard, notably so in the London Season, when the orders increased inordinately and the working hours did too.

Hannam certainly had the traditional 'baptism of fire' in his introduction to working life in the metropolis. He would have been working in rooms with a temperature of over 30 degrees Celsius; he may only have had five or six hours off work per day. In addition to this, the cooks and bakers would also often deliver the bread and cakes they had made. He would have been exhausted at the end of his working day. However, the work gave him something which would be valuable to a copper: a knowledge of working-class life and manual labour, along with a basic idea of the layout of London streets and boroughs, so essential to the daily work of 'knowing the patch' and having a comprehensive notion of the spread and nature of the great city around Scotland Yard.

It has to be said that Hannam's first employment would not have been all hard graft. Just after the First World War, for instance, there was a bakers' and confectioners' week held at the Royal Agricultural Hall in Islington, and the showpiece for the pastry cooks' art was a wonderful detailed model of the Menin Gate. The reporter for one paper wrote: 'Pastry cooks and chefs from all over the country are eagerly vying with each other in a huge bread and cake-making competition ... Every kind of pastry and sweetmeat from five-tier wedding cakes to humble but delicious lumps of toffee is on view.'

But young Hannam had other ideas for his future. It will probably never be known why he joined the police, but there is no doubt that in the inter-war years it was a career with a bright future. In addition to advances made in forensic science in the first decades of the twentieth century, there were organisational plans in progress. The top brass were of the opinion that, once the hard post-war years were sorted and matters returned to normal in the streets, the police force would need restructuring. There had been a crisis in 1919 when there had been industrial problems in the constabulary; this had gradually been worked out, and at the time when Hannam joined the ranks he would have earned around 35 shillings a week. Later, in the late thirties and the Second World War years, he would have earned a little over 40 shillings a week as a third-class sergeant, climbing to almost £300 per annum as a second-class inspector.

There was also a problem with gangland at the time when Hannam joined as a young constable. In the aftermath of the First World War there had been widespread poverty and unemployment. This had been exacerbated by the horrendous flu epidemics of 1918 and 1919, and it had become clear to returning Tommies that there was no 'home fit for heroes' awaiting them. Crime was an option, and it was seen by many as a legitimate business opportunity. The thinking was that, if one were to start a business, then a firm was needed – a gang, in fact. There was strength in numbers, and a gang offered each member the chance to use his special skills, whether that was as a driver or a safebreaker, as 'muscle' or as 'brains'.

But the 'science of detection' is not only evident in the laboratory. The logistics of running a detective branch entails much more than theory and experiment. In London and across the country the organised crime networks, together with the increasingly brutal and ruthless robberies and killings in the streets after the First World War, when so many men acted desperately in an age of mass unemployment and deprivation, meant that the Yard needed new strategies. Most notable of all the initiatives taken by the 'new men' in the ranks was the creation of the Flying Squad. This was formed in 1919 specifically to combat that post-war flood of crime. The idea was that a small, centralised body of officers would work in particular areas, each under the direction of a superintendent. The central concept was a variation on the use of an independent unit, working with its own methods, set apart from mainstream policing. At first, horse-drawn wagons with spy holes had been used (hired from the Great Western Railway) but these were later replaced by two Crossley Tenders and then by much faster vehicles. Before the First World War, detectives had the measure of the criminal geography of the metropolis; it has been claimed that in 1910 around 95 per cent of crooks operating in

London and the Home Counties were known to Yard officers. There was also a well-established network of informants and a rapport existed that would create immediate lines of enquiry when a crime was committed. Only after the Second World War was a directive given signalling a change of attitude in the top brass. Detectives were forbidden, according to Stanley Firmin, to 'have any truck with crooks or others living on the fringe of crookdom and ordered under threat of dire penalties to discontinue at once their visits to those places where crooks were likely to congregate'. When a fresh crime wave, fronted by many new faces, began, there was a serious problem. Many villains were ex-servicemen who had adapted their military skills to activities on the wrong side of the law.

The epidemic of crime expressed itself largely as armed robbery. The squad assembled to combat this had to have a number of expert drivers, and men with other particular talents. The first force consisted of 180 CID men, and there were branches of the squad at five locations around London. Smaller squads of a dozen men were the staple of the work, and this group included a mix of sergeants and constables. The first name given to this famous cadre of men was the Mobile Patrol Experiment, used until 1920, but thereafter it was known as the Flying Squad. The force was repeatedly streamlined over the next decade, and by 1929 it was given an establishment of forty officers, led by a Detective Superintendent of C1, Central CID.

After the Second World War it became known as Branch C8. After the Crossley Tenders were brought in, replacing the horse and wagon, the next innovation was a radio transmitting station placed on the roof of Scotland Yard, which used Morse Code. By 1927 new cars came in: Lea Francis convertibles with a top speed of 75 mph. Brooklands motor track was used to train the special drivers who would work with the squad and their cars became known as Q Cars because of their interchangeable number plates. After the new cars had suffered badly by being rammed by villains' vehicles, a sturdier yet still fast car was brought in, the Invictas, having a top speed of 90 mph.

Most notable in the work of the Flying Squad was the way they related to the old-school crooks, the ones who resented the amoral and gun-centred antics of the new breed of villain. The 'career criminals' were more likely to become informants and develop a rapport with the squad officers who regularly worked their territory. As this paid dividends for the squad in its high clear-up rates, and the old-school crooks in its elimination of their rivals, the system suited all parties very well.

The squad was the most suitable counter-measure against a particularly nasty and desperate racetrack war that went on in the 1920s, principally involving gangs from different parts of the country. After the First World War, racetrack bookmakers provided easy money for protection racket crooks. Billy Kimber was a main player, leading the Birmingham Boys gang; they had an alliance with the Leeds Gang, and as time went on their main enemies were the Sabini brothers from Clerkenwell. Kimber was based in London, so his rival Charles 'Dardy' Sabini was not far away from him. When Sabini and his four brothers looked towards the racetracks for some regular income, there was bound to be trouble. The two outfits would be taking each other on, and it was up to the detectives of the Flying Squad to prevent trouble whenever they could.

In 1921 there was a major confrontation after the Derby. Detective Inspector Stevens was there, observing the two factions, so they decided to meet elsewhere. On the road from Epsom, there was a blunder: the Leeds Gang, friends of the Kimber men, were attacked, on the assumption that they were Sabini's men. There was a bloody fight at Ewell and Stevens rushed to the scene. A charabanc used by the attackers was spotted parked by a public house and the police took away the spark plugs before cornering the villains. The hero of the hour was Sergeant

Dawson, who faced the whole gang; as they came at him, he pulled out a revolver and said he would shoot the first man who tried to escape.

Of course, Sabini had come out well; his enemies had mistakenly attacked each other. But matters were still extremely serious in the gang wars. There were murders in 1924, and a crowd of racing thugs attacked a police officer at Victoria station. The protection racket was thriving; by the mid-1920s a bookmaker was not safe unless he paid at least £20 a day to the crooks. After a particularly vicious confrontation, the Flying Squad were given a direct brief to take on the gangs more aggressively. At this point a detective of considerable fame appears on the scene: Fred 'Nutty' Sharpe. He was a tough rugby player from South Wales and he had been hardened working down the pit. In his police career he began as a constable in London, working in the East End. After being spotted as a likely candidate by Wensley, the CID chief, Sharpe was assigned to the Flying Squad. The decision was a good one.

Sharpe was tough and fearless. All varieties of crooks at the tracks were his prey, from muggers to pickpockets. Tales were told of his pretending to be a drunk in order to attract robbers, and then he would take them on with his fists. As several writers have said, only the most reckless of gang members would refuse to obey his command. The first to attempt recalcitrance, either by word or deed, would be in trouble, seriously injured and sorry he tried to cross the man.

As was common practice, squad specialists were called to help outside the city as well, but it was on the tracks that they were in demand, and this continued for decades. Most famous of all was the episode of the Hoxton Mob in 1936, when some bookies linked to the Sabini gang were brutally attacked by Hoxton members. Nutty Sharpe heard of the plan and he was there at the course when it went down; most of the perpetrators were taken to trial and sentenced, with some locked up for three years. This was at Lewes Assizes, and it marked the victory of the squad over the gangs on the tracks. Sharpe became head of the squad for a short period before his retirement in July 1937. The one statement that most sums up this hard and intelligent officer is his comment on the secret of accurate knowledge: 'The more crooks a man knows intimately, the more he knows about the underworld and what it is thinking and doing, then the more likely he is to be of use.'

*

For detective work, the inter-war years were largely a time when several practical aids and innovations came into use, even down to the introduction of the 'murder bag' by Sir Bernard Spilsbury. This bag contained the various items needed at the scene of crime of a murder. Spilsbury and Chief Inspector Percy Savage had been required to handle the flesh of a body in decomposition, and this brought home to Spilsbury the need for officers to use rubber gloves to avoid sepsis. From that detail, a whole panoply of protective items was introduced.

Into this atmosphere Hannam entered in 1927, ready to learn. After his training, the career record shows a string of commendations, the first one coming in October 1931, when the note on his record has, 'Commended for action in case of larceny'. In March 1933 he was promoted to Detective Sergeant and was now a CID man.

The initial training, as a constable, would have been at Peel House, Victoria, which had opened in 1907 and continued until the sixties. His service record notes that he was precisely 5 feet 10½ inches. That specific height was important at a time when the public expected their bobbies to be physically imposing. As he had joined the Met in 1927, he missed the establishment of the new college at Hendon by seven years. But we know that he learned on the job, both as a young constable and of course in his first months as a detective constable.

Obviously, detective work, as with law and medicine, teaching and many administrative professions, requires probationary time on the job. But we do know that when he was older, Hannam was consulted regarding police training. After his retirement, he received a letter from a fellow officer thanking him for the loan of some printed training material, and the writer followed up with, 'I think your comments on the various pages are well merited. They show clearly the difference between doing the job and commenting on it by what one reads.'[1]

Between June 1932 and 1940 he was active in a number of small-scale cases encompassing housebreaking, cycle theft and fraud. In July 1937 he was commended for his 'ability in effecting an arrest'. By 1938 he was Detective Sergeant 1st Class, in the thick of the wartime offences. In those early years he was starting to use the skills he had learned in his training at the Police College. We know a great deal about that training, as Hannam entered the profession at the time when detective work was under intense scrutiny. In the early thirties, a committee was formed to prepare a report on detective work and procedure, and their report was issued in 1938. The group of twenty-five men, chaired by A. L. Dixon, presented their findings to the Home Secretary, Sir Samuel Hoare, and were extremely thorough. Hannam's training may be gleaned from this.

The report was in eight volumes, and it covered everything from local work to communications and forensics. An important point with Hannam's career in mind is summed up in this section on the issue of probation: 'In the course of our enquiry we have found some difference of opinion on the question whether a constable who has been selected for detective work and who has completed his course of training should be on probation as a detective for any given period.'[2] In effect, Hannam and his peers would have had that probation. There was an unofficial period for such observation and reporting.

The training was intensive and extensive. The extreme thoroughness of the approach may be seen in the material relating to the taking of photographs, for instance. Here, the report has several pages of diagrams and photographs, showing a meticulous approach to the procedure. But far more interesting is the material relating to the crucial skills of interviewing and interpersonal behaviour in investigation.

In between the study of statistics and guidelines, Hannam would have been well informed on topics relating to procedure and record-keeping, but it is noticeable that the material regarding the human side of things is slender compared to that dealing with facts and information.

Percy Hoskins, who was later to become something of a bugbear in Hannam's work on the Bodkin Adams case, wrote a book on this training in 1940, and as he was a press photographer he included plenty of pictures. This book, *No Hiding Place*, is a profile of the Yard at this time. Hoskins sums up the attitude to the aforementioned training, referring to a raw recruit known as X: 'The first thirteen weeks of his new career were spent at Peel House training centre acquiring the rudimentary principles of police work. Almost before his course was over, X was asking, "How do I get into the CID?" He was promptly informed he would have to spend an allotted time in the uniform branch.'[3]

Hoskins summarises the process of making a detective: 'The CID recruit is taken from the uniform branch and made a temporary detective-constable for one year. During this period of probation the would-be sleuth is put through the mill, and on the theory that it takes an old dog to teach a puppy, he is sent on the rounds with an experienced detective.'[4]

It is not difficult to imagine young Hannam around the time of the outbreak of war in that learning situation. He was destined to be learning the basics of the work while the Blitz was in full swing around him.

The young detective in training was the product of the new system initiated by Lord Trenchard, who had been transferred to the Met from the RAF, tasked with overseeing reform after the troubles immediately post-war related to police pay and conditions of service. He proposed the establishment of the Hendon Police College, described by one writer succinctly and fully as a place 'to catch the most able young constables, by competitive entry or recommendation for accelerated promotion, and to recruit well-educated young men from public schools, colleges and universities, all with the promise of immediate appointment to the newly created rank of Junior Station Inspector after their two-year course. The course itself would concentrate rather more on physical fitness and character-training than academics.'[5]

Hannam's early work as a sergeant is reflected in the first commendations. Just before the war, in late 1938, for instance, he was involved in one of those extraordinary cases which defy explanation. The headline in the *Derby Evening Telegraph* says it all: 'Man with £15000 a Year Steals Eggs.' Hannam had hidden himself in a shop owned by Kenneth Garvey, Westminster, to observe the behaviour of William Barnett, a man who called in to buy a bottle of beer every evening; Barnett stole six marked eggs while the owner's back was turned, and was arrested. The wealthy shoplifter said, 'It is very silly of me. Will this mean ruin?' The man was on the board of a number of firms, and previously he had been a mining engineer in South Africa. His lawyer said, 'His companies bring him in over £1500 a year, and it does seem on the face of it one of the most inexplicable cases one could imagine. This gentleman has brought irreparable ruin upon himself.'

A Harley Street specialist was called as an expert witness and comments were made on the accused's problems with memory and concentration. The result was that the case was dismissed with a 20 shilling fine imposed.

In January 1939, Hannam was involved in detecting a case of fraud. This was the case of William Wayte, thirty-one, who was given a jail term of nine months for obtaining goods by false pretences in West End shops. Hannam told the Old Bailey, 'For the past two years he has been living a Jekyll and Hyde existence in the West End. He describes himself as a journalist. Between 1927 and 1934 at premises in Fleet Street and later in The Strand he ran a business styled *Oxford and Cambridge Magazine*. Before June 1928 there were accumulated deficiencies [from his whole career as an entrepreneur] in the region of £10,000.' After this the man somehow acquired rooms in Bruton Street, Mayfair, running other journals, and at Queen Street he ran a firm called Hunting and Racing Ltd. This came to an end in January 1938. The result was that he was in court, facing Mr Christmas Humphreys, to whom he insisted not a penny had gone into his own pockets.

In 1940 and 1941 there were a number of thefts at the Air Ministry, and Hannam was one of the first officers in action at Adastral House, Kingsway. The thefts were discovered after a box containing confidential papers was checked and found to have been searched and disturbed. A £5 note had been hidden inside, and an investigation revealed that amount had been stolen from an employee. Hannam reported on this in court when William Freeman was convicted and given a six-month jail sentence.

The Air Ministry seems to have been one of Hannam's special duties, as he was the man who brought in a very suspicious character who had been stopped in a corridor at the Kingsway headquarters. This was Martin Ozamis, who was there with no pass, and who was ostensibly seeking work as a pilot. A supervisor, Herbert Roberts, first accosted Ozamis and started asking questions. The man's answers were very strange, as he said that he wanted to see the contracts for the ferry service. He was referring to the Atlantic Ferry Service to Canada. The provost was called in and he was told that Ozamis claimed to have worked on that ferry service in 1934.

Ozamis was then interviewed by Hannam, and he said that he had undertaken flights to France and Spain. Mysteriously, a strange cablegram was found on Ozamis, which read, 'L.C. Department of Justice, Washington. Trying telephone you are President Roosevelt from Spanish Embassy, London. Reply immediately c/o Charing Cross Western Union where I can telephone you.'

The mystery still remained when the magistrate convicted him under the DORA regulations (Defence of the Realm), specifically for 'being found [in a place] ... for a purpose prejudicial to the public safety for the defence of the realm'.

*

It was October 1944 when Hannam was first involved in a major murder investigation. It was the time when V2 rockets were over London in spite of such reassuring measures as the standing-down of the Home Guard. Fortunately for posterity, this case was on the books of Dr Keith Simpson, the famous Home Office pathologist of the war years, and he wrote an account of it in his memoirs. To add even more detail, Dr Simpson's secretary was the celebrated novelist and literary historian Molly Lefebure, whose book *Murder on the Home Front* provided the material for a successful television drama. Consequently we know a lot about this case, a homicide often referred to as the Kempston Ballast Pond case or the Gribble case. Molly Lefebure became a good friend to Bert Hannam, and it is clear from her account of this case that she and the detective knew each other well, and met on several occasions.

Molly was born in 1919 in Clissold Park, and her father was a senior civil servant who worked on the NHS establishment with

Beveridge. She attended the North London Collegiate School and then studied in France before going to St Godric's Secretarial College in Hampstead. She then started work as a reporter and met John Gerrish, whom she later married. It was at this point that she became secretary to Dr Simpson, who was not only the pathologist for the Home Office but also head of the Department of Forensic Medicine at Guy's Hospital. Her memoir of the work with him in wartime London provides one of the best narratives of pathology and investigation in the midst of the Blitz. Simpson chose this specialism at a time when such forensic experts were thin on the ground. In his memoir he wrote, 'I was not the only newcomer in London but one of a trio referred to as "The Three Musketeers" by the police, and privately, by the press also. The other two were Francis Camps and Donald Teare.'[6] Simpson summarises the wartime situation Hannam was experiencing very neatly: 'During the training periods of 1939–1943 there was a steady flow of rapes (some with strangling or other violence), of assaults (some fatal), of abortions and infanticides, all arising from the changes of life that were thrust by service conditions on ordinary people.'[7]

Kempston, a parish in Bedfordshire, had a population of around 10,000 in the 1951 census. There was no census in 1941. There were barracks near there, and a ballast pond had been formed. This is a feature usually created in areas near shipyards or dockyards, a place where stone ballast was dumped. This was necessary when guns and masts were removed from or added to vessels, at which point ballast had to be used to compensate for the loss or increase in weight, with excess ballast being dumped in such ponds.

The story began in August 1944 when a dog, nosing in vegetation, found the body of Robert Smith, aged twenty-four, at Kempston near the ballast pond. Simpson and Molly were called. The local police had said it looked like a murder scenario; they had found the body of a young man, severely battered and wounded, with multiple wounds to the body and head. The body had been in the undergrowth for some time, as there were maggots busy on the rotting flesh.

But one detail was soon revealed which made identification possible: a torn-up photo had been found not far from the body, and a policewoman recognized the girl in the picture, connecting the dots from there. The dead man was Bob Smith. He had been working for a local firewood merchant called Gribble. There was a determined and thorough search of the scene for more evidence, and as this was going on enquiries were made by Inspector Beveridge and his young sergeant, Bert Hannam. The son of the firewood merchant, Ken Gribble, told the detectives that he had arranged to meet Smith at the ballast pond but that Bob never turned up. That could have been accepted, but a watchman had seen a bicycle left out in the lane not far from the scene of crime, and he had taken the bike to the police station, where it had soon been identified as belonging to Bob Smith.

Again Gribble was questioned, and he denied any knowledge of a meeting with the dead man. The case needed forensic work, and Simpson knew that the murder weapon would almost certainly have eyebrow hairs adhering to it. The search for the weapon thus began. Simpson's forensics determined a time of death which matched the meeting that probably did take place between the young men, so suspicions were aroused regarding Gribble. What was needed then was an opinion regarding the manner of death, and some insight into whether or not this was a murder.

Simpson studied the wounds, and when the police found a sawn-off bough and took it to the laboratory, things fell into place. As Simpson wrote: 'I told the police at least four blows had been struck, and the third was a knock-out. I thought that the fourth had been delivered when Smith was already lying on the ground, helpless.'[8]

It looked like murder, then. There was serious damage done to the eye-socket and to the jaw. The dead man had raised an arm to defend himself, but blows from the bough had rained down hard and strong and he had been beaten to the ground. As for young Gribble, who was only sixteen, he tried to provide an alibi, given by his girlfriend, but she caved in and the truth was out: the two men had met at the ballast pond in early August. Finally, Gribble, in the company of his family, who begged him to tell the whole story, confessed to having a desperate fight with his friend – a fight which had started when they fell out over money.

The victim, it transpired, had taken some time to die, and Gribble had not run off to try to find help. That fact would look very seriously wrong in court, and a murder verdict would be almost certain, but at least Gribble had done one thing: he had tried to revive Smith before dragging him into cover when at last he despaired of bringing him back to life.

In the midst of all the investigation into the crime scene, Hannam had been busy with the local men in the search for more evidence for the forensic lab. The crucially important evidence was dental. DCI Beveridge insisted on some teeth being found, and those teeth were lost down a drain at the mortuary. Without Molly Lefebure's account of events, we would know nothing about these details of the case. She gives a vivid picture of the whole police investigation process. The novelist in her comes through in her descriptions of events and places. She gives the impact of the first arrival and the officers involved: 'Chief Inspector Peter Beveridge was a large man with a fresh complexion, youthful blue eyes, shy smile, a very firm handshake and a quiet voice which expressed great authority.'[9] Then she has to take notes, and there is Bert Hannam: 'Behind him, to my utmost relief, stood detective Sergeant H. W. Hannam, whom I had met several times before and knew as an understanding ally.'

In that first phase of the investigation, Molly saw, from close up, Beveridge and Hannam in action: 'From time to time during this resume of the facts, Mr Beveridge turned to Sergeant Hannam, who had taken a small sheaf of notes from his briefcase. Mr Hannam checked these notes with his chief's information.' In this way, we have a vivid account of the two detectives working together.

The search of the area around the body began, under Beveridge's direction, and the body was taken to the mortuary, which was not far from the crime scene. Molly's description of the mortuary is powerful and darkly informative. Simpson was disgusted at the poor conditions of the mortuary, and as the search for the missing teeth went on he had the body moved to his own lab in London. As Simpson and Beveridge went through a steady and thorough re-creation of the events of the fateful fight, Hannam and Molly Lefebure took their notes.

It transpired that Gribble had spent around ten minutes trying to revive his friend, and that fact saved his own life, one could argue. Gribble was a mere teenager, and though technically he could hang if a murder verdict was reached, recent events had shown that leniency was more than likely applied in cases involving youthful killers. In 1931, a teenager in Waddingham, Lincolnshire, had slaughtered his aunt and uncle at their home. The death sentence had been passed on the boy, but the Home Secretary received an appeal. One of the lawyers in the case had told the press, 'I am sure that public opinion cannot approve of the death sentence being passed on boys of this tender age when there is no likelihood of it being carried into effect.'[10]

The trial took place at Leicester Assizes. The argument in support of murder was that Gribble had continued to viciously attack his opponent, and that this attack went far beyond any simple retaliation. But the lesser offence of manslaughter was given as the result of the jury's deliberations. One newspaper report put the result most succinctly: 'Gribble … had not the slightest intention of killing Smith and would not have struck him had Smith not attacked him.' The sentence was three years in prison.

Molly Lefebure gave the most powerful summing-up: 'Sordid details, dirty scraps of old newspaper and torn odds and ends, a drain to be delved into, a patch of waste land to be searched again and again…'[11] Yet, as she rightly concluded, most criminal cases involve such 'grind and dogged sweat'.

Bert Hannam's boss, Chief Inspector Beveridge, was promoted, and as Molly pointed out, still thinking of her friend Bert, 'as for my old friend Detective Sergeant Hannam, at the time I am typing this he is a mere few miles away from me, down river at Richmond, conducting enquiries into a double murder.' Reading between those lines, we may see just how much Molly appreciated the human side of police work; Bert's humour made him approachable. The Gribble case highlights Hannam's abilities and experience at a turning point in his career. He had proved himself in the great melting pot of criminal chaos during the war, and had been so adaptable that he could work in a range of contexts which were the domain of the Yard.

In a period of around twenty years, Hannam had moved from police constable to detective sergeant and was rewarded and recognised for his particular (and rare) abilities as an investigator. Working with Beveridge, he was learning how to act when leading an investigation. To a general reader, the question of how a detective learns his or her skills may never be prominent in the mind, but common sense shows that learning by observation, by taking orders and by asking questions, is a process by which experience develops, and in a very different way from in a lecture room or from textbooks.

Molly Lefebure's memoir contains much that, by sheer inference, puts the spotlight on Hannam's attainments by the last year of the war. Her account of the Gribble case shows him as being somewhat in the background, joining in with the team behind Beveridge with no dissent or complaint; he did the dirtiest jobs, along with other staff. Molly's hints at their friendship suggest something much more trustful and easy than a purely perfunctory professional relationship. Her comments make it clear that he was totally reliable, in a world which was increasingly chaotic and suspect as a world war raged around them. In her account of the case, Hannam is depicted as an essential part of the investigation, though he is much closer to her than others; her notes show a man taking care over all location-based details.

He was also a master of methodical procedure in investigation. The tranche of recruits to detective work just after Hannam's graduation experienced the full innovative regimen of the new Police College, the training outlined in Percy Hoskins's book *No Hiding Place*. Coming into maturity as a sleuth at this time, Bert Hannam acquired just the right workable balance of theory and experience to equip him for any task that might be thrown into his path. Even the popular pulp crime magazines showed an understanding of a detective's work: its boredom and routine as well as its drama. The training manuals might have been thorough and detailed, and the routine station work might have been dour and repetitive, but it was all groundwork. How else could he have produced such massive documentation later on, in the major cases? No, there is no doubt that by around 1946, when the dust was far from settled across bombed London, Bert Hannam was a seasoned, blooded professional, able to cope with whatever orders came his way. This was just as well, for he was about to face one of the most complex criminal personalities in the annals of twentieth-century homicide, and a case which was to push him to the limits in its tortuous alleys and avenues, well off the main highway of standard investigation.

3

A CONFESSION FROM THE NICK: THE WALTER ROWLAND CASE 1946

Two years after the Gribble case, Hannam was called into the investigation of a Manchester murder which led to a strange and questionable prison confession. He was to be caught in the wrangling of an official enquiry, a focal point in the 'last-chance saloon' position of a man who had been on another murder charge long before he confessed to this one. There would be a strange and uneasy hiatus as everyone waited for the results of an investigation into the man's confession from the prison cell. This is one of Bert Hannam's most controversial cases: that of Walter Rowland, who was twice convicted of murder. Even more sensational than Rowland's criminal record was the drama that was to unfold inside prison walls, involving Hannam in a tough assignment. It was to be a case typical of a murder investigation, with a trial in which the past record of the accused is far from easily understood or assessed and the present situation is complicated by medical or psychological factors which defy analysis, or at least undisputed analysis. It was to be a case which led to a stream of learned studies, mostly concerned with using the murder in order to further the contemporary debate on capital punishment.

This was also the case that taught Hannam that persistence and small-scale local enquiries tend to bring results. The killer turned out to be a friend of the victim, with the murder taking place in a close-knit local community where tempers had frayed – one of the most common homicide scenarios, in fact. We know from memoirs that Hannam was a key member of the investigation team, with his presence leading to a major contribution as a truly bizarre development changed the balance of the whole case.

Hannam had entered the world of investigation beyond London to find something that was no more than a fist-fight that ended in tragic death. It was to prove to be the usual fodder of a homicide case: sordid, filthy and revolting, with a puzzle at the heart of it. This was more in the character of the killer than in the circumstances of the crime. Hannam's role was once again to tread the streets, knock on doors and interview people connected with the events of the crime. But there was going to be another element in this information gathering, and it must have been Hannam's first large-scale experience of the complexity inherent in a murder investigation. As a first-case exemplar, it confirmed the view – often repeated – that a murder is a squalid, dirty affair with dignity and humanity stripped away with the material clutter around the remains of the victim. It also has to be stressed, given the attitudes of the time on 'ladies of the night', that the victim was a prostitute, and so Hannam found himself moving around in the seedy, nocturnal and shadowy world of sex for sale in the ruins of war – in a landscape of destruction.

*

Walter Rowland is a complex character to weigh up. In 1934 this miner from Derbyshire was sentenced to death after he killed his two-year-old daughter by strangling her with a stocking. In his appeal statement, Rowland had said, 'I am innocent and a victim of circumstances.' In short, the prosecution, it was felt at appeal, never really proved the crime, but nonetheless persuaded the jury of Rowland's guilt. The evidence was seen as purely circumstantial. In the summing-up, the judge said, 'It is perfectly clear that the little child has been killed by somebody, that she had been left in the charge of her father ... and she was murdered while her mother was elsewhere.'

Rowland's life stands comparison with the most complex and contradictory in the annals of British crime. In 1975, Henry Cecil published a book-length account of Rowland's career and crimes, and this opened up his full life story to scrutiny. But it is useful here to trace the earlier life of Rowland, over the years up to his first conviction for murder.

Rowland was born in 1908 at New Mills, Derbyshire. From his teenage years he was hard to handle. At first he tried engineering, and that did not work out; the next move was to join the Royal Tank Corps, but he was discharged as being medically unfit to serve. This was only the beginning of a long period of personal crises, risky adventures and dangerous brushes with the law. In October 1932 his danger to the public became crystal clear when he committed highway robbery; by this time he was married, but that did not stop him making advances toward another woman, which he did when his wife was present. Not only did he try it on with a stranger, but he also tried to take his own life in public. In front of his wife, he drank some Lysol, severely burning his stomach; he was only saved by a nurse who happened to be present.

It was a week after this attempted suicide that he approached a parked car in which a couple were sitting peacefully in a country lane. Rowland, ostensibly armed, threatened to fill the car with lead unless he was given money, spinning a yarn about having a starving family. He was given all the cash that the man had – 13 shillings. The papers who reported this crime once solved also picked up on an earlier report concerning Rowland: that he had once tried to strangle a girl. This was clearly a man who should be in custody, and he was given a year's hard labour at the Derbyshire Quarter Sessions. The judge told him that, had the case been heard at an Assize Court, he would have been given penal servitude. That would have been the kind of sentence that would break a man's body as well as his spirit.

Then, in 1934, came the first murder. The story broke in March of that year. It was a truly horrendous crime: the murder of his own infant child. This was his little daughter, Mavis, who was born in February 1932. Almost exactly two years later, the baby had been murdered. Rowland was sentenced to death, his appeal against his sentence being dismissed, but he was later reprieved. He came out of prison in 1942, the middle of the war, and he served in the army until 1946. To a modern analyst, so much of his behaviour conforms to that of a psychopath, and one with a strong current of narcissism running through his personality. He was a drifter geographically but also mentally, with an unruly nature.

Then came the second murder charge, in October 1946. This time the scene was in Manchester, where the body of prostitute Olive Balchin was found on waste ground in Cumberland Street. She had been battered to death with hammer blows to the head. Rowland was in Manchester and had a previous murder conviction, so he was questioned; he claimed to have been at 36 Hyde Road at the time, where he was lodging. Indeed, his presence there had been noted, and he had been signed in on the night of the murder, but that was overlooked in the investigation. Rowland did admit that he had been with Olive, however. He also made several rash statements to the police, including the fact that he had a venereal disease and that if it had been Olive who had given it to him then she deserved what she got. Everything was pointing to him as the killer. He was identified on parades, and the times of his stated movements meant that it was just possible for him to have been with Olive at the time she died. He was charged, and forensic evidence painted a very bleak picture for him – it was noted that in his trouser turn-ups there was a cluster of materials that matched the substances at the crime scene.

Rowland was sentenced to death, but then came the stunning news that a man in Walton gaol had confessed to the crime. This was David Ware, and he wrote: 'I wish to confess that I killed Olive Balshaw [that spelling is important] with a hammer at the bombed site in Deansgate, Manchester on Saturday 19 October at about 10 p.m. We had been in a picture house near the Belle Vue stadium.' This was to prove tantalisingly ambiguous and problematic for the detectives, who went to check the man out. Bert Hannam was part of the team that went to work on David Ware and his confession. He was also to be an important figure in the later inquiry, which began as Rowland was locked up for the crime.

Amazingly, Ware gave a comprehensive account of the night at the pictures, with lots of details that seemed convincing. Surely this meant that, like the famous Christopher Simcox, Rowland was going to be saved from the noose a second time? Perhaps not, for Hannam was of the opinion that the details Ware had mentioned could be gleaned by anybody passing by. He did not accept the tale as convincing, and thought that Ware, being of unsound mind, was fantasising. Hannam reported that he had found a number of press cuttings with details relevant to the case. He wrote: 'In two of these cuttings the victim is said to be "Balshaw". In one of these cuttings published within a few days of the discovery of the body the name is said to be "Balshaw".'

The real fascination of the Rowland case lies in the odd coincidences and questionable actions of both Ware and Rowland in their alleged movements around the time of the murder, which took place around 11.00 p.m. on 19 October. Rowland's movements were strange, and his entire lifestyle most peculiar. His parents' house was not so far away, at New Mills; he went there to take laundry for washing. However, he himself stayed at low-quality lodging houses, Salvation Army hostels and anywhere else where he could find a bed. There is no doubt that he was a violent man, and he would today be labelled a psychopath, as he was clearly a restless, dangerous outsider with extreme mood swings, a lack of empathy for others, a streak of narcissism and no ability to build loving and stable relationships.

Olive Balchin was battered to death, and the hammer used, along with the brown paper it was wrapped in, was left at the scene. Although there have been conflicting interpretations of the evidence, the facts remain that three people selected Rowland in identity parades and he openly confessed that he had gone in search of Balchin, whom he already knew from previous sexual encounters, thinking that she had given him a sexually transmitted disease. He brashly told police that he would assault her if she was responsible.

Lined up against that evidence are these details: there were no prints of Rowland's on the hammer; none of his clothing had blood on it, apart from a small trace on one shoe, while the nature of the hammer attacks entailed considerable blood spatter; and there were no witnesses. It had seemed as if Rowland had an alibi, and that is where Bert Hannam first figures in the tale. Rowland said, in interview, that he had stayed on the night of the murder at a particular address; Hannam investigated and found confusion as to the dates in the record book there. The result was that Rowland's movements on the night of the murder still made it possible for him to have done the deed in between bus journeys to various locations.

Hannam worked on the enquiry into Ware's confession with John Jolly, who was appointed to lead. Jolly's report was issued on 25 February 1947. The task was to look very closely at David Ware's confession. The first statement of confession was made on 22 January that year and this is the wording:

Sir, I, David John Ware, wish to confess that I killed Olive Bagshaw with a hammer, on a bombed-site in the Deansgate, Manchester, on Saturday October 19, about 10 p.m. We had been to a Picture House near the Belle Vue Stadium earlier in the evening. I did not know her before that night. I wish this to be used in evidence and accepted as the truth.

While the investigation was in progress, the Court of Appeal heard Rowland's lawyer's argument and turned it down. The main problem was that their Lordships Goddard, Humphries and Lewis had interpreted Ware's confession as something which would lead to a situation in which Ware was under trial at a court of appeal. Lord Goddard summarised: 'The court has come to the conclusion that this appeal must be dismissed; but as a question has arisen here with regard to an application to call the evidence of a witness who is alleged to have made a confession with regard to this crime, and the court has refused to allow that evidence to be given, the court will put their judgement into writing ... That judgement will be given at an early date, but the appeal is dismissed.'

Nevertheless, Jolly and Hannam continued with their questions. Ware had made two later statements after that initial confession, so now the police team were dealing with three statements, made from within prison walls, by a man who knew he could hang if his confession was believed. In his final statement, Ware retracted his confession: 'I do remember reading in the paper about the peculiarity of the buttons on the coat worn by the murdered woman.' He also finally said, 'I would like to say I am sorry I have given the trouble I have and I didn't realise the serious consequences it might entail had the confession been believed.'

This led Jolly and Hannam to hold absolute confidence in their reading of events, and to that effect, an identity parade was called. Ware was lined up with ten other prisoners. The three key witnesses were called and all three failed to recognise Ware. The Ware confession was beginning to look very flimsy. Hannam now reported one of the other principal reasons why Ware's confession was dismissed: 'I have inspected numerous press cuttings published prior to the committal of Rowland. One of those includes at the request of the police a photograph of the coat worn by Balchin and comment is made of the distinctive nature of the buttons upon that coat. In at least two of these reports the price paid for the hammer is quoted, and one sets out in thick type the finding some distance from the body of the piece of paper in which the hammer was wrapped...' In other words, all of Ware's information, including some fine detail, could have been obtained from press reports. Hannam had done the fieldwork required.

Of course, when a man's life was at stake, all these measures had to be taken. One small detail which emerged later would have soon shifted all credence regarding the confession: the fact that Ware had deliberately marked a coat with bloodstains while in the prison workshop. This crazy move, which he later effaced by removing the stains, shows how far he was prepared to go in order to fabricate 'evidence'.

Walter Rowland was hanged at Manchester on 27 February 1946 by Albert Pierrepoint. He was not as fortunate as Simcox, but between them they had three reprieves and just one hanging.

*

There is a strange coda to this story: on 10 July 1951, David Ware tried to kill a woman in Bristol. He had bought a hammer and had tried to batter her to death. He was found guilty but did not hang due to a verdict of insanity, instead being committed to Broadmoor. In fact, he took his own life there, hanging himself in his cell in 1954. Was Rowland innocent after all?

Arguably, the definitive study of the case was in print in 1975, from the pen of Henry Cecil. *The Trial of Walter Rowland* covers all the trial, appeal and investigation material, and Cecil's conclusion is strongly worded: 'I have come to the clear conclusion that, in spite of Ware's confession and in spite of the fact that four years later he attempted to commit a similar crime, and in spite of the criticism that has been made of the verdict, the case of Rowland calls for no further enquiry. He was plainly guilty.'

In spite of the apparently definitive treatment of the case by Cecil, there is no denying that the Rowland case continues to attract attention from crime historians; in the sixties and seventies, when Penguin Publishing were promoting any number of social investigations across all the humanities subjects, their 'Crime Specials' were specifically designed to stir up discussion and controversy, and it was in this line that they published Leslie Hale's *Hanged in Error* (1961). Cecil dismissed Hale's argument, but nevertheless it ends with Hannam at the centre of the narrative: 'The register at the lodging house where Ware claimed to have spent the Saturday night from about 11.15 onwards had been inspected by two police officers after Ware's confession ... Inspector Hannam went to see it in late February. He was told that the book had been destroyed. The report does not state whether an explanation was asked for or supplied.'

This incomplete account of the checking of the record book caused controversy over the case to continue, when in fact, as Cecil explained, some other records relating to Ware show wrong (and smudged) dates which make it almost certain that Ware's recorded dates of staying in Manchester were wrongly transcribed.[12]

Nevertheless, the true crime genre and its readers love a good controversy, and they also long for cold cases to be revisited. As for Bert Hannam's part, it has to be said that fate always had him marked as a man with a career swamped by the most sensational criminal investigations. Detectives arguably thrive on that (and who wants a tedious case anyway?), but such a life offers few days off, and as detectives have often testified, a murder investigation fills up one's life, night and day, until the affair is resolved.

But in the mood of the fifties, when there was pressure in Parliament to abolish or at least suspend the death penalty, there was a rush to print on cases in which there was doubt as to the condemned person's guilt. Sidney Silverman, who was to be the main influence behind the abolition of execution in 1965 via the Murder (Abolition of Death Penalty) Bill, wrote a long essay on the Rowland case in a collection of writings specifically commissioned to study the cases of potential miscarriages of justice in recent years. In his essay, huge tracts of the trial process are reproduced verbatim.

In his conclusion, which offers succinctly the opposite view to that of Cecil, he asks plainly whether Rowland, Ware or neither man murdered Olive Balchin. 'No-one will ever know. The jury found him guilty on the evidence they had heard. They did not know that another man would three times confess to the murder, and then withdraw his confession in a statement plainly untrue in some material parts. They did not know that the man had a long history of mental illness ending in his conviction, on his own confession – this time it was believed – of an attempted murder of exactly the same kind...'[13] The problem with this is that Ware had admitted to having a fixation on committing a murder of this nature, and it was more a case of his mental obsession than any link with Olive Balchin which led him to try to commit the Bristol murder. Silverman preferred to believe in the innocence of Rowland, one might argue, on the strength of Rowland's powerful oratory in court. This was an aspect of the case which impressed Cecil too.

Rowland had said, in letters to a friend and to his parents, that he was innocent, and in such terms that a high level of emotional content comes through, and Silverman was surely influenced by this. For instance, Rowland wrote to a Mr Keymer, 'You know that I have a clear conscience and you have my sacred word at this time when I am too near to death's door, that I am an innocent man.' History teaches us that condemned persons tend to protest their innocence with strong and emotive rhetoric, and Cecil argues that this is the case here.

There is another factor here: in the author's possession is a copy of the book in which Silverman's essay appears; the copy was previously owned by Mr Jolly, who led the investigation into Ware. Fortunately for posterity, Mr Jolly has supplied margin notes in the book. His notes concern the possible alibi for Ware on the night of 19 October, when he allegedly spent the night with a prostitute at an address that was a three-minute taxi-ride from Piccadilly. Silverman wrote, 'By irresistible inference that he slept in Stockport not on the 19th but on the 20th Mr Jolly has been misled by thinking that, in the passage Mr Jolly quotes, Ware was talking of the 19th. He was not – that was the night before. It is a pity that the book was destroyed.'[14] Silverman adds that Mr Jolly considered the last statement by Ware. This was in the report to the Home Secretary, and Silverman comments that Ware was clearly not telling the truth as to his whereabouts. In other words, he was not accounted for on the evening of the murder, but only on the night after the murder.

My copy of the book has Mr Jolly's response. He wrote in the margin, 'It was my mistake in statement. The Home Secretary would not allow alteration.' But of course, it has no impact really, because there was no forensic evidence connecting the corpse or the crime scene to Ware. There is also the matter of there being no fingerprints linking Rowland to the hammer. Silverman wrote, 'It may be assumed safely that Rowland's prints were not there. But were any fingerprints there? Was the hammer examined for fingerprints? Were they too smudged to be reliable? We do not know; no evidence was offered. It is a curious omission.' Mr Jolly's response is, 'Ridiculous?' Regarding Ware in this context, it is significant that the Director of the Preston Forensic Laboratory made a statement: 'From my observations in this case, I am of the opinion that the description given by Ware of his attack on the deceased is not consistent with the facts in this case.'[15]

Silverman's argument is based on the assumption that Ware's basis for confession was sound. But as Hannam showed, the prisoner in Walton Gaol was in thrall to a fantasy, a delusion in which he took a life in the manner in which Olive Balchin died.

The noose resolved the Rowland case. The public executioner, Albert Pierrepoint, carried out the execution. He had just returned from Germany, where he had seen several Nazi war criminals into eternity, and his memoirs suggest that he did not consider the Rowland case to be worth any comment. He skips the whole affair, which is strange when one considers the singular and extraordinary life and deviant adventures Rowland had. For Pierrepoint it was just another hanging, and he was especially busy as he had just become a pub landlord, taking over the Help the Poor Struggler public house near Oldham. He was too busy to note much about this Derbyshire man and his highly controversial death, which was to remain a bone of contention as a steady flow of books and articles were published. The Ware participation here may have been a total fantasy. It may have all been part of his twisted ideas about being like Rowland. Comments on the man's sanity suggest that he was so mentally fragile that he could have convinced himself that he actually was Rowland, spinning the imaginary narrative from within his prison cell.

Bert Hannam, for his part, had played a supporting role in conducting investigations to back up the Jolly report, but it was the kind of good police work that closes cases and satisfies top lawyers. By the end of the war he had learned a great deal about sleuthing; he had surely perceived that much of it is about dogged perseverance and sheer physical stamina. He had become adept at logging information, interviewing suspects and playing a valuable part in the essential teamwork of Scotland Yard operations. He was soon to take a leading role in a very different aspect of post-war crime, and his wartime years had taught him well. He was ready for any test of his mettle.

4

PROBING DOLLAR RACKETS
1947

Sometimes a major crime is not evident in a single villain, but in the hearts and minds of a multitude, and this does not have to take the form of a riot or a revolution. Just as often it can be about pound notes and promissory notes, not firearms and assaults. Hannam certainly learned this in 1947. In such cases the offences may be too numerous to count, and a desperate search begins – not necessarily to grab any culprits by the collar, but merely to understand the transgression.

In that year, after being deeply involved in murder and manslaughter cases, Bert Hannam found himself in demand for work on a very different kind of crime: the white-collar world of illegal speculation and money or securities transfer. The type of crime emerged just after the war, when major economic factors in the commerce between nations and the shadow of enormous war debt wrought confusion and cast a gloom on the British treasury.

It was in early 1947 that the general public would first become aware of something worrying going on in the world of major finance, when papers had announcement such as this, in a regional Scottish daily:

HOLIDAYS ON THE CONTINENT

Alleged evasions of currency regulations

For some time the Director of Public Prosecutions has been considering evidence supplied by the Treasury in regard to serious evasions of the currency regulations. This concerns British people on holiday on the continent. It has now been decided to issue summonses in almost 100 cases.[16]

What was going on? The ordinary citizen would have been very worried. Not that so many were able to holiday abroad, but the wealthy would have suspected that something nasty was in the wind as far as their little world was concerned. Why was the government worrying about holiday money?

The answer had its roots many years before 1947, the point at which Hannam was to be involved in such investigations, and the police were to look far beyond just holiday money. This was something that impacted on the national economy in the widest sense.

In the early 1930s, the Great Depression had a profound effect on Britain; there was unemployment and consequently extreme poverty in many areas. To be unemployed in 1931 was to be without money and food at a time when there was no welfare state. The fear of the workhouse still loomed in working-class families. However, there was a recovery. Despite the huge national debt after the First World War, the recession did not last so long, with growth picking up from 1934. But first the country had to survive the crisis of 1931, when Prime Minister Ramsay MacDonald and Chancellor Philip Snowden applied severe spending restrictions. The pound was the problem. It was overvalued, so in 1931 Britain left the gold standard, devaluing the pound. Interest rates fell quickly, and against the dollar the pound devalued to 28 per cent.

When the Second World War came along, of course, economic matters were mostly on hold, and one issue so neglected was exchange control. Basically, in a free market where speculators may buy currency in one place and then put it into another market where it may be sold at a profit, or where securities and investments may be handled in the same way, an individual economy has no central knowledge nor control of its credit and its resources. In normal circumstances, Britain would give considerable time and thought to the control of its economic situation, but when America entered the war, and the defeat of Hitler and the Axis powers was paramount, the control of international exchange slipped.

Recent access to the Bank of England records for this period shows that exchange control was of great concern from the end of the First World War to the eve of the Second World War, and reports by the London Exchange Committee give an insight into the situation by the middle of the Second World War. This needs to be explained before Hannam's work in this affair is recounted.

In 1915, exchange control was challenged, as the report makes clear: 'The policy adopted was founded on the conviction that the benefit derived from any avoidable curtailment of the traditional freedom of British monetary and commercial intercourse would be rendered nugatory by the blow to British prestige.'[17] In other words, the mindset of Empire and late Victorian ideas of free trade were still powerful. But a sub-committee pressed for exchange control. In plain terms, this means that, if all transfers of capital and currency are known and controlled at supervised rates, the economy as a whole will be understood, restrained and communicated in statistical returns which 'take the economic pulse' of the nation. A situation without control meant that 'there was no co-ordination of control in different exchanges; and while sterling was pegged at a discount of 2% in New York, it ultimately fell to 25% in Amsterdam.'[18]

In 1929 the Bank of England began to intervene, and after the abandonment of the gold standard in 1931 they had to become more aggressive. An account was instated to log the fluctuation in the exchange value of sterling. Well before the outbreak of war, the bank applied some controls. The archives explain this: 'Broadly speaking these disallowed: purchases of foreign securities in foreign markets, and of foreign currencies except for definite imports under contract; the import of securities and subsequent remittances abroad for the proceeds of their sale; sterling advances against foreign balances and forward market operations.'[19] This is as good a description of the framework for a black market as you might find. In these categories we may see the basis of the speculators' trading, which happened without exchange control; and some of this, of course, was in the hands of criminals.

Foreign assets belonging to British nationals, including gold, would have to be brought home. It was specified that this had to happen after the outbreak of war. What in fact happened was a widespread suspension of such actions. The report of the committee described exactly what the situation was when the Yard were called in to help the Treasury investigators after the war: 'Powers should be taken to control any export of gold or transfer of sterling balances, while gold held by foreigners before a certain date should be exported under licence.'[20]

In layperson's terms, the gold standard links the actual amount of gold bullion owned by a bank to the amount of currency issued and circulated. The two should tally, albeit notionally and ideally. But now, off the gold standard, inflation was the enemy. The amount of sterling in circulation has to be controlled lest inflation spiral; what could happen when it did was fresh in the memory for Europeans after the hyperinflation that hit Germany after the First World War.

Of course, the war with Nazi Germany brought about a hiatus. In 1939, one official at the Bank of England explained the fundamental fear behind the work of this committee: 'The Bank proposed blocking of non-residents' sterling immediately on the outbreak of war as the most complete measure to avoid haphazard and embarrassing withdrawal of foreign-owned balances and at the same time to prevent their use in the black market.'[21]

After the war, when these concerns were raised again, it was the black market which was targeted by the Treasury and then by the Yard. But the situation was far more than simply a black-market run by villains. Anecdotal and oral history, together with my own experience living in that time, shows that in the 1940s and 1950s there was an almost universal habit of hoarding cash: paper money, kept at home or spent within the hidden economy of unlogged transactions, was seen as being far more reliable than money in the bank, at least by ordinary people. The experience of war had taught the ordinary citizen the important lesson that self-help and survival go together like 'a horse and carriage' in the words of a popular song of the time.

The economics of war on the Home Front, and the sheer terror of having one's own home and neighbourhood under attack, led to a mindset of communal assistance but also, paradoxically, of self-preservation. Harsh economic necessities impinged directly on life, even into the 1950s. It was in the interests of the government to perpetuate the wartime make-do-and-mend ethos and to slim down the appeal of having money. It was under these circumstances that in 1948, Arthur Bryant, writing in a periodical, stressed a certain attitude: 'A country's happiness is not measured in material wealth, but of its people's contentment. A diamond tiara, a "luxury" plumbing outfit, a large bank balance, are only valuable so far as they bring content of mind to their possessors. Otherwise, they have no more value than a stone, a swamp or a dream.'[22] The truth is that ordinary folk longed for an escape from the tough times. In 1947, when the new legislation attempting financial regulation was passed, the slogan selling Johnnie Walker whisky was:

Time Marches On!
Midway between the Future and the Past,
I can look back to bygone 1820.
Today may be austere, but it won't last –
Here's looking forward to the age of plenty![23]

Food rationing continued until 1953. There were clothing coupons, and virtually everyone had to wear 'utility' clothing in the post-war years. Style and fashion were in the world of make-believe for most people. In 1945, for instance, the *Daily Mail* announced that 'clothes coupons may have to last longer'. It reported that, 'appealing for more cotton operatives at Oldham yesterday, Sir Stafford Cripps, President of the Board of Trade, said we had reached a point in our supply of cotton cloth where it was doubtful whether we could maintain the ration of clothing even at its present rate.'[24]

The fact is that in 1947, the Bank of England and the Treasury were, in the language of the time, in a terrible funk. They had come to realize that the hidden economy was beyond both their definition and their influence. There was too much paper money under mattresses and stuffed into walls. There was too much taken abroad, too. Legislation had to be introduced to control this, and it arrived in the shape of the Exchange Control Act, which followed on from the Exchange Control Division, previously established in 1939.

This Act was to deal with securities, re-designation of accounts, legacies, emigration, cheap sterling, shipping and many other matters. There was even a need to look into relationships in the UK with the American film industry, and Hannam was to figure in that matter. As explained earlier in this chapter, the Exchange Control panel had been meeting and reporting for many years, but by 1947 there had to be direct action. This was 'an Act to confer powers, and impose duties and restrictions, in relation to gold, currency, payments, securities, debts, and the import, transfer and settlement of property'.

Gold and foreign currency were a principal concern. The first diktat was that no dealing in currency should take place except with the participation of authorised dealers; this was followed by a crystal-clear description of what the government wanted to stop:

> Every person in or resident in the United Kingdom who is entitled to sell, or to procure the sale of, any gold or any foreign currency to which this section applies, and is not an authorised dealer, unless the Treasury consent to the retention and use thereof or he disposes thereof to any other person with the permission of the treasury.[25]

We can see the results of this in the popular press. Letters and parcels which might be suspected of containing pound notes or other valuables were to be liable to be intercepted, whether they were leaving or entering Britain. As early as March 1947, a Yard man had been called in to work with the Treasury investigation team: he was Chief Inspector Wilfred Tarr, and Hannam was to be his number-one assistant. The *Evening Telegraph* gave the essential information for the layperson, ignorant of the complex economics involved: 'A number of the prosecutions will involve notable people. The majority of the summonses will be heard at Bow Street ... Treasury investigators found that the amount of money was so large it was bound to have a serious effect ... Last night Chief Inspector Wilfred Tarr of Scotland Yard went to France. He had with him a special dossier connected with people suspected of spending long holidays on the Continent at a rate of expenditure far above the £75 limit.'

By August of the same year, it became known that Hannam was involved in what one paper called 'super-snooping'. In one report we have an account of a side of Bert Hannam which has rarely been acknowledged:

YARD MAN TO PROBE DOLLAR RACKETS

Detective Inspector Herbert Hannam, who is being sent by Scotland Yard to the United States to investigate latest developments in currency rackets, is one of the financial experts in the Yard. He is also described as Scotland Yard's best-dressed detective. His friends say he looks more like a stockbroker than a detective. He is assistant to Chief Inspector Wilfred Tarr, the Yard's chief money expert. Hannam's knowledge of finance rivals that of many of the best financiers in England. He also has a good knowledge of languages and recently accompanied Chief Inspector Tarr to Belgium, Switzerland and France to investigate currency offences. He is in his forties and is one of the most popular officers at the Yard.[26]

The report also mentioned that Hannam was involved in looking into property purchases in the States using illegal high-price dollars.

Wilfred Tarr was a remarkable character. Financial investigation was not his only skill; even after official retirement, we know that he and another former Yard man, Sergeant Foster, took part in the enquiries regarding the Northamptonshire murder of Mr and Mrs George Peach in 1956. One of the most discussed unsolved murders of the fifties, it took place at Ashton, near Oundle, where gamekeeper George Peach and his wife Lilian were killed at home. Four years after their deaths, and prompted by a phone call telling police that 'someone at a fair in Tottenham knows something about the murder', Tarr came out of retirement to lead a second enquiry. Eventually he had to issue a statement of defeat: 'No further development.' But it says a great deal about the man that he would get back to work in such circumstances.

As mentioned earlier, Hannam's work in this case would involve the American film industry; this relates to the Anglo-American Film Agreement, which had been established in 1938. The *Times* report explained, 'The Metro-Goldwyn-Meyer Corporation of America have entered into a joint agreement with the Gaumont-British and Gainsborough organisations for the immediate production of films in this country. The first to be made will be *The Lady Vanishes* by Mr Alfred Hitchcock ... The films will be distributed in this country by the American organisation, and in return for the concession the British companies will be given a right of way into the American market.'[27] This had been complicated in August 1947 when the Treasury imposed a 75 per cent customs tax on all film imports. The result was that the US applied a boycott, and British film production was left to try to fill all the slots in a typical industry year solely through their own productions. The risk to the industry generally was massive. This situation was not ameliorated until early 1948 when Harold Wilson, President of the Board of Trade, made a constructive move: 'Talks led to an[other] Anglo-American Film Agreement in March 1948. In return for an abolition of the duty ... the American studios would again export films to Britain.'[28]

This latest development, which saw sterling shifted to Hollywood as Brits moved and took capital with them, impinged on the brief given to the Yard men. The actual investigations were kept hush-hush, but in Parliament much wider issues than the financial were raised and debated. Hansard reported on this, for instance, from Mr Oliver

Lyttelton: 'It is a good thing that the world should be told about the way we live, about our full democracy in this country, how some of our institutions work, of the impartiality of British justice and so forth.'[29] What many had come to understand, by the time that Tarr and Hannam set to work with the Treasury, was that this whole subject encompassed ideology and aesthetics as well as finance.

As far as the press were concerned, the whole business of exchange control smacked of something nasty and un-British. As the *Courier and Advertiser* wrote, 'Our Customs officers have, in the last month, been stripping outgoing British travellers even of rings from their fingers, for fear they should sell them abroad. This inquisition exceeds anything practised on the Continent, and even a Socialist commentator admits the common criticism that "Britain is going National Socialist" contains unpleasant truths.'[30]

Finally, perhaps the clearest way to grasp what was going on in 1947 in the ranks of the Treasury, and their worries and stresses, is to envisage a typical scene that could have been noted anywhere in the country at that time. A person runs a small business; he has a safe in the tied house of an employee. The cash takings may be kept there for a month or longer, as he is not a regular at his bank. In fact, he always takes aside a certain percentage of that cash for his own savings. If thousands do this – and they did – then the cash they all accrue is part of the 'hidden economy' beyond the control of the authorities. Calling in the Yard men may seem an extreme measure for getting a handle on this, and searching holiday luggage and letters abroad for pound notes may seem ridiculous, but how else, in a world without computers and the internet, could surveillance and regulation be effected?

The image conjured by this scenario is that of a once great empire, which has almost been brought to its knees by a costly war, desperately trying to gather in the kind of material security which the Victorian and Edwardian worlds were founded on. The gold was not in the vaults, backing all the trade; it was in the unruly and unpredictable sterling, darting around the world, influenced by all the bad habits of a wartime black market.

Bert Hannam and his boss were in the struggle for that control, and while at times it all seems ridiculous and desperate, at other times it has something heroic about it. The economists sitting on the committee for currency regulation had experienced decades of suggestions, resolutions and frustrations. With the war behind them they could finally act, and Scotland Yard was their only ally.

It may seem to be a truly gargantuan task to snoop on the country's mail, but in fact, throughout the war, thousands of workers had done exactly that. Documentary films exist which show huge halls lined with workers opening mail. The same facility was used by the Yard to snoop on the exiled Duke and Duchess of Windsor when they were suspected of liaising with Nazis during the war.

To understand Hannam's work in the years 1947 and 1948, it is necessary to appreciate that there was a type of desperation in the Treasury which had not been anticipated. It was the result of a familiar story: the committees had met, warnings had been given and a string of eggheads from the world of economics had spoken, but matters had been deferred because there was a war on. When in 1947 the legislation did come along, it was a puzzling mixture of panic and surreal comedy. There emerged that very British custom of officialdom mixing with individuals' rights and customs. We can almost imagine the Donald McGill postcards showing the ruddy-faced and overfed day trippers complaining as their luggage was inspected or their mail ripped open and their pounds sterling taken away.

But of course, there was a bigger picture, and what is staggering to contemplate today is how quickly Bert Hannam learned his role when assigned the work with Wilfred Tarr. They were two of a kind: dedicated, determined and perfect for a job entailing a delicate mix of toughness and common sense. The bigger picture was undoubtedly worrying for those in positions of responsibility. The war had left Britain with debts of over £3,000 million. When the government had initially arranged the bulk of their loans from the USA, everything had been dependant on the pound sterling being controlled in markets, and easily convertible. By 1947 that matter was more urgent than ever. Today, there would be more personnel involved in such investigations, with staff other than police officers. But Hannam was moving in a world in which extreme specialism had not yet percolated into every profession.

There is no riot or revolution, then, in this phase of Bert Hannam's life, but the 'hidden economy' may well be a greater enemy to national stability than gangs or dissidents; in this case, though, there is nothing sensational. There is always the feeling, when thinking of mail searches and bank accounts being scrutinised, that Orwell's *1984* was not too far away in people's minds. Orwell was writing that book in 1948, and in this world of mail checks and confiscations he saw the future so horrifically imagined in his novel.

5

THE TEDDINGTON
TOWPATH MURDERS
1953

One of the most celebrated dicta of forensic science is the Locard Principle: every contact leaves a trace. In this notorious murder case, a crazed killer brutally raped and killed two young girls and left ample traces. But compared with today, when every effort would be made to preserve any location where there might have been contact by the killer, back in the 1950s the securing of the crime scene was not so well organised. The 'traces' had to be hunted down by teams of men. In this case the evidence was thoroughly hidden, but when eventually found it was to prove crucially important. For Hannam it was the first prominent case in which he was lead man. It was now his turn to apply what he had learned from Inspector Beveridge and others; his training was about to kick in. He would need it, for the nature of the crime was enough to upset the toughest constitution. The killer had used an axe.

As the immediate post-war years rolled on, and rationing continued along with the rebuilding, Hannam would have found that his profession was considered to be glamorous. This was the golden age of detective fiction, and as the real Scotland Yard men set to work on the often sordid and brutal killings across the land, the fictional sleuth was in his heyday. J. B. Priestley, who had provided the immensely popular *Postscript* radio broadcasts during the war, in 1949 gathered together a collection of short essays on his favourite pastimes, and one of these was 'reading detective stories in bed'. He wrote, 'After the newspaper headlines, it is refreshing to enter this well-ordered microcosm, like finding one's way into a garden after wandering in the jungle.'[31] It might have been escapism for some, but for many there was nothing amusing or recreational about serious crime. News reports usually shattered the image offered by popular depictions of crime. Not that Bert Hannam had any time for the popular tales.

There was no sense in which Bert Hannam would have seen his detective work as taking place in any location but a jungle. The human jungle of his patch, where murders were a daily occurrence, entailed the most unsavoury, revolting and demanding work one could imagine. Throughout his career, much of his work was similar to the nasty investigation at the Ballast Pond in Kempston, where he and his colleagues were searching drains and fields for the remains of a human body.

Murder, he had surely learned through tough experience, is a dirty business from start to finish; any variety of homicide demands that the detective immerses himself in the darker depths of human depravity. The work is also something that leaves an imprint on the investigators, from the nastiness and mess of the crime scene and the corpse to the potential for trauma and nightmares that the harsh reality engenders. The Kempston enquiry had contained all this, and its narrative had none of the supposed glamour and excitement of the penny dreadful magazines.

The same was to be found in the Teddington Towpath case of 1953. That year is memorable for many events, most notably for the coronation of Queen Elizabeth II, and in fact this crime happened as those national celebrations were in full swing. It was the year of the first espresso coffee bar, a time when a quarter of households owned a television. The G-Plan furniture designs had arrived, and such developments saw a growing common interest in modern style and the opening up of popular culture to teenagers. In the gloomier world of serious crime, it was the year in which the multiple killer John Christie was hanged, three years after another man, Timothy Evans, had been wrongly executed for one of the murders. As a result, debate was raging around the topic of the death penalty.[32] Nevertheless, for the time being the punishment for murder was death at the end of a rope, and the murders in Teddington did nothing to diminish the majority view that such killers have to be removed from the earth by a state-appointed executioner.

*

On Monday 1 June 1953, the dead body of sixteen-year-old Barbara Songhurst was found close to Teddington Lock; she had been stabbed several times and thrown into the river. The previous day she had gone out cycling with her older friend Christine Reed, eighteen, and they had been seen out late, around 11 p.m., on the path. Barbara was the kind of girl who had to be socially involved: open, friendly and communicative. She had acted as a pen-friend to servicemen, and the *Daily Mail* reported that she enjoyed male company, quoting her father's words: 'At 10 a.m. on Sunday Barbara came home, dressed in her blue jeans after having stayed the night at Christine's home. She said she was going to cycle to Brighton with Christine ... My daughter had many boy-friends. One of her friends who was in the British army in Germany wrote to her regularly. He used to send her love poetry.'[33] Naturally, when Mr Songhurst found one such poem under his daughter's pillow, some of the words written there gave an indication of the girl's nature: 'I will be honest with you. I do not know where you live or work, but I was told about you from a friend who lives near you.'

Readers of the *Daily Mail* piece, as well as officers starting to investigate the case, would thus be clear that young Barbara was perhaps so amiable and outgoing that she was leaving herself vulnerable to exploitation – or even attack – from strangers. The international nature of her correspondence was immediately studied by Hannam as he took over investigation. One report ran, 'Chief Detective Inspector Herbert Hannam of Scotland Yard, in charge of enquiries, was last night examining evidence which indicated that Barbara had pen-friends covering almost the whole world where British troops are stationed.' She had been in the habit of sending her photo to anyone who wrote. It comes as little surprise that the first potential suspect was a serviceman, an American stationed at nearby Bushy Park. The man in question was 'an Indian', and one witness said of the night before her death, 'I was at the dance and saw this Indian. He was very dark and handsome in his way.' This had been at a bebop dance at York House, Twickenham Town Hall.

Many officers on duty for the coronation were drafted in to work in the search along the path, because Barbara's friend Christine was still missing on 2 June. As the search for Christine and any forensic evidence progressed, details began to emerge. Barbara had been severely battered and raped, as well as being stabbed in the back.

By 2 June draglines and magnets were being employed by the police searching the stretch between Teddington Lock and Eel Pie Island. A double murder was suspected when two pairs of shoes were found. It was soon realised that the place where Barbara had been dumped implied that the killer thought the tide would take her body out to sea. In fact, a second ebb tide after the killing had left the body exposed to view. There was no sign yet of the girls' bicycles.

More details came out about the girls. *The News Chronicle* reported, 'Blonde Barbara Songhurst of Princess Road, Teddington, was a chemist's shop assistant; dark Christine Reed of Roy Grove, Hampton, worked in a factory. Barbara's father says she was "clever" Christine's mother says she was "backward".' Quite why the paper felt it should publish these details is puzzling. More information was given to the press as Chief Inspector Rudkin of the Murder Squad began to reconstruct the crime. In the middle of the war, Rudkin had been involved in sorting out the 'bombing with bank notes' affair, in which Hitler's industrial experts had flooded the UK with forged British banknotes. This became known when a man called Alfred Naujocks was arrested in 1944 and revealed the nature and scale of the forgeries. A forging factory had been created at Sachsenhausen Camp, and the cash was used to buy supplies from neutral states. Rudkin and a crack team of men were sent to check this out and gather information.

As he became involved in the Teddington business, Rudkin must have thought that he was fated to sleuth around water; in Germany he found that £10 million in banknotes had been thrown into the River Enns. Rudkin's men had to explore the river depths at Toplitzee. Now, here he was, working in rivers again, combing the place for evidence with Hannam.

Rudkin explained to the *News Chronicle* what had probably happened: 'He could see signs of a struggle near Teddington Lock – a mile away from where the girl's body was found. Barbara had fought desperately for her life; in her nails the pathologist found fibre from a man's sports jacket. And the grass near Lovers' Towpath was trampled for thirty yards ... Her shoes had been pulled off as the murderer dragged her near the towpath. Nobody living nearby – in a housing estate or a camping site – heard any sound of a struggle.'

Barbara, the middle child of nine children, had only just bought her bike, for £17, the previous week. When she met her death, she was wearing a white blouse, blue trousers, white socks, and had a necklace around her neck. She also wore a wide black belt with a square clasp buckle. The search for Christine, who was just 5 feet 6 inches tall, intensified. Hannam and his squad searched through the night. The hunt for the Asian serviceman petered out, and there was a desperate need for some kind of lead in the case. An area of long grass was scythed and police asked questions across a wide area.

Working with Hannam was George Lyle, then a detective sergeant at Richmond. He was later to lead the CID team at Wimbledon. He was one of the founding members of the Met's Drugs Squad after the war. Hannam had top detectives working with him, then, with Lyle and Rudkin being the most prominent. But despite all their skills and experience, they needed a break. At last, on 6 June, this came, with the sad discovery of Christine's body. She had been stabbed ten times.

At the end of June, the – apparently major – breakthrough came when a man was arrested on suspicion of committing assaults on two women in Surrey. This was Alfred Whiteway, a married man who was living with his parents, separate from his wife. He had a bicycle and had been seen on the towpath. He put forward the alibi that he had been visiting his wife at the time of the killings, but excellent forensic work by Dr Keith Mant had proffered some evidence: blood on Whiteway's shoe.

Hannam was the man faced with 'breaking' Whiteway and extracting a confession. But there was something else. Mant, who had been in the Royal Army Medical Corps in the war and had been given the terrible task of interviewing Nazis accused of undertaking medical experiments at Ravensbrück Camp, made some notes on the 'blunt instrument' involved in the horrendous assault; however, they needed clarification. Only when a crass act of foolishness on the part of the police was uncovered was the necessary forensic information revealed. This was the discovery of an axe in a patrol car as it was being cleaned. A constable had taken the axe home from the scene of the Towpath murders, and later placed it in his patrol car. It was vital evidence, of course. The police officer who had taken it home had used it to chop wood.

Hannam extracted the confession from Whiteway. The killer had roamed the area on his bike, looking for victims. He said that he had raped and attacked Barbara, thinking she was alone, but then he saw Christine, at a lower level, by the lock, screaming. He attacked and killed her too.

But then came the controversy which dogged Hannam throughout his police career. At the Old Bailey trial, Whiteway insisted that his 'confession' had been concocted by Hannam, and that he had never said he killed anyone. Defending Whiteway was Arthur Prothero, who instructed Peter Rawlinson. These two made a formidable alliance in court.

In a murder trial, the focus of attention is sometimes drawn fully to the procedural work of the police or the administrative staff of the criminal justice system. This necessarily entails close scrutiny in the battle between defence and prosecution, as each party strenuously attempts to find weaknesses in the witnesses for the other side. The Whiteway trial was one such case, and it would not be the first time that Bert Hannam found himself defending his corner, in spite of his meticulous attention to detail in his work.

The trial had its fair share of drama. Naturally, after the fiasco of the axe being lost and then found – in a police car – the officer responsible for taking the axe home was subject to a certain amount of pressure in court. The man in question was PC Arthur Cosh, and the stress was too much for him. *The News Chronicle* gave the headline that no officer would have wanted to read: 'Policeman Faints in Box at Murder Trial.' This was on 27 October, and the report, by George Glenton, gave a very interesting impression of Peter Rawlinson and his methods. This interchange shows his populist approach:

Rawlinson asked: 'Why did you put it [the axe] away in your locker and not report it?'

'The practice among drivers is that anything found in the car is claimed by the driver driving it.'

'Is that the practice and you don't report it?'

'I have never found anything before.'

Amid laughter, the judge asked, 'You are not suggesting that if a man leaves a jimmy in a car the officer claims it?'

'No Sir,' replied PC Cosh.[34]

In the more popular true crime books, Hannam has been painted very black with regard to this affair. Frankie Fraser, for instance, in his comments given to James Morton, wrote, 'Hannam may have got away with it that time but he come [*sic*] a cropper with the case over that doctor…'[35] This is a gross exaggeration, and a bland acceptance of a press campaign to smear Hannam.

James Morton, writing for *The Law Society Gazette*, commented that 'the prosecution was something of a mess' in the Whiteway trial.[36] He points out that Hannam was supposed to have a photographic memory and that this didn't appear to be in evidence. Hannam, in court, was well aware that the constable's borrowing of the axe was extremely embarrassing for the police and their investigation. Now here he was, facing examination over the contents of the alleged confession. Morton sums up what happened when Rawlinson went into action: 'Rawlinson put Hannam through a gruelling two-day cross-examination on the methods he adopted in drawing-up the signed confession. He opened substantial gaps in the officer's evidence and Hannam never forgot the experience.'

A huge headline in *The News Chronicle* reflects the pressure Hannam was under: 'I Did Not Sign that Towpath Confession, Whiteway says.' This was all about the alleged confession. Whiteway had told his defence counsel, Michael Havers, that he had never made a statement to the police. The press report giving Christmas Humphreys' words was printed in bold: 'You are alleging that these two officers [Superintendent Hannam and Sergeant Hudson] forged that statement and committed perjury in putting it before the jury?' Whiteway simply stated that he never said what was alleged. Later, Hannam faced Rawlinson and the interchange was blunt and direct: 'At the hearing the day before, Mr Rawlinson suggested to Superintendent Hannam that the alleged confession was completely manufactured. Superintendent Hannam replied, "That is absolutely untrue."'[37]

Rawlinson, who read Law at Cambridge and served with the Irish Guards in the war, later became Baron Rawlinson of Ewell. The Whiteway case was his first to attract major press attention, and it made his name. He later worked with Melford Stevenson in the Ruth Ellis trial in 1955, and in 1962 he became Solicitor-General. The man he teamed up with to defend Whiteway was also a force to be reckoned with: Arthur Prothero. He lived to be ninety-nine and in time became Solicitor of the Supreme Court and a member of the Council of the Law Society. He was often to be found in print offering opinions on court procedure, and he felt strongly about the issue of electing to be tried by jury. He expressed this in 1966, for instance, when he wrote, 'It is always difficult to deal with a general allegation. It may well be that the defendants ... have elected to be tried by jury and he [the solicitor] has thought this course unnecessary...' But in the Whiteway case, he showed his mettle when in fact there was overriding forensic evidence to pinpoint Whiteway as the killer of the two girls.

One thing is certain: Sergeant Hudson was a very effective back-up for Hannam in court. He was cross-examined and the circumstances of the confession were broached. The questioning enlightens us as to what happened:

Detective Sergeant Hudson yesterday was asked by Mr Humphreys if Whiteway dictated the statement smoothly or jerkily.

Sergeant Hudson replied, 'My impression was that it came out in fits and starts.'

Sergeant Hudson said that Superintendent Hannam stopped Whiteway twice while he was writing and spoke to him. The first time he stopped he said to Whiteway, 'It is important that I write down the exact words you say, and therefore I don't want you to speak too quickly.' The second time was when Whiteway asked Superintendent Hannam, 'What else do you want to know?' Superintendent Hannam replied, 'Nothing, Whiteway, only what you want to tell me.'

In spite of Hannam's ordeal at the hands of Rawlinson and Prothero, it took the jury only thirty minutes to find Whiteway guilty and he was sentenced to hang. Frankie Fraser perhaps expressed the situation most powerfully: 'Here was a man on trial for his life and people said that Rawlinson had gone in a bit strong against the copper Bert

Hannam … he didn't half lay into him … it didn't do Whiteway any good…'[38]

There is an interesting coda to this case. Twenty years after the Whiteway trial, Hannam wrote to *The Times*, making allegations against Rawlinson, who was then the Attorney General. Hannam alleged that, as there had been claims against a small minority of criminal lawyers of fabricating evidence, he felt he needed to dig up the past. The fillip for this was a speech by Sir Robert Mark, the Metropolitan Police Commissioner, who had referred to 'shady lawyers'. Hannam made it clear that he was not accusing Rawlinson of being such a man but he did make reference to a statement of Rawlinson's in a letter that 'we knew they [the arguments] were all untrue but they were my instructions' – in other words, his actions in the trial were part of a brief from someone else.

What transpired was a long meeting between the old adversaries, and in Rawlinson's reply we have an insight into their relationship and that tough 1953 trial: 'My letter to him congratulates him on his conduct … I have a copy of that letter and it is the only letter I wrote to Mr Hannam. My letter thanked him for understanding the difficult task which had faced me as defending counsel. Nowhere does there appear in that letter the words "we knew they were all untrue but they were my instructions". There are other misquotations. I did not congratulate him on his composure, nor did I express regrets.'[39]

There was then a meeting in which matters were resolved, and *The Times* reported soon after that Hannam had admitted to confusing two letters. Rawlinson issued a statement and so did Hannam. The latter wrote that 'The memory of twenty years allowed me to combine the contents of both letters.' This belated accusation is important because it presents something familiar in Hannam's character: it suggests that he had massive archives, and perhaps kept everything from his career.

If the comment about him having a photographic memory is based on fact, then perhaps he had such a capacious memory that over time texts were conflated and mixed, and he imagined some statements.

Whatever the truth of this, it is surely indicative of some kind of burning resentment that Hannam should feel, twenty years after the event, that he needed to express such a criticism. The Whiteway case had cut deeply into him. He was, after all, the man who took the flak after a horrendous error regarding vital forensic evidence. Throughout Hannam's police career, controversy was drawn to him, and he always appeared to relish a certain amount of give and take; the courtroom drama held no fear for him, and he moved easily among the solicitors and barristers with whom he had to deal. The Teddington Towpath case brought out his fearless confrontation with various types of authority, and it seems now, with hindsight, that while he did not openly invite the cut-and-thrust of power play, he was usually somewhere nearby when trouble was brewing.

The intense courtroom struggle regarding the confession and the behaviour of the police as claimed by the killer looks, with hindsight, like the desperate and rather unprincipled gambit of a defence team eager to win by any means necessary. What the ordeal did for Hannam was prepare him for the most extreme, relentless attacks from the best of the defence lawyers; it has always been said that Hannam could easily have been a lawyer, and the records suggest that he coped admirably when on the stand. We have to conclude that he more than held his own under cross-examination and perhaps even relished the combat, the meeting of minds. The Towpath case was always going to be a special challenge for him, since the unfortunate appropriation of the axe by the constable. In a world in which the crime scene and its contents were not as sacrosanct as they are today, the police paid the price for sloppiness and complacency, and the man who had to face the music was Bert Hannam. He came out very well.

This had been one of those investigations that a detective faces when he or she has reached the stage of maturity and sophistication required to survive intense 'grilling' by lawyers who are out to shame or degrade, or at least to embarrass. Bert Hannam was well up to the task, and of course he knew very well that the error over the axe in the car required some kind of compensatory assertion of police efficiency.

What lingers is a press photo of two police officers searching the undergrowth by the towpath, with a huddled crowd of bystanders behind. Placed together, uneasily, are two things – the recreational nature of the location, and the thick undergrowth and what it hides. The result is the ambiguity laid on extreme violence that such dark deeds engender.

Hannam had moved into the limelight. From now on, thanks to Mr Rawlinson, he was to be the one the press searched for and bothered, like flies around a horse in the field.

6

CONSPIRACIES
1955

There is something about the word 'conspiracy' that puts a dark shadow over any discussion or description. Looking back, as in our case here, to an era now mired in obscurity, the word suggests a threatening alternative to whatever picture the historian tries to paint. In the example of the British police, and in the context of the 1950s, the notion of a conspiracy is even more unsettling; to place the word in the heart of something which serves to protect is to seed a poisonous flower in a bed of beautiful roses.

In this instance the conspiracy was part of a long-held public perception of the police as corrupt. What certainly did not help was the media's affection for that 'C' word, reinforcing a common view that 'coppers were all bent' and that you couldn't trust the police to look into their own shortcomings. The issue goes on and on; in 2017 Sir Peter Fahy, former Chief Constable of the Greater Manchester Police, called for an independent body to investigate alleged police corruption, and the Independent Police Complaints Commission, formed in 2003, was replaced by the Independent Office for Police Conduct in 2015. These facts make it clear that 'corruption', in whatever form, has always been, and is even now, a major concern for the police. Back in the 1950s, Hannam was the individual called in to establish fact from fiction, and to attempt to identify actual instances of corruption.

A police force exists to secure, provide comfort and reassure. A century before the events to be described in this chapter, the police detective force (the CID) was very new, only coming into being in 1842. Its members struggled to perform their duties because they worked undercover, much in the way that spies do. To the general public this seemed underhand, nefarious, duplicitous. To work in plain clothes was to hide, to submerge oneself in a dishonest craft. By the 1950s, however, the police had established themselves as a pillar of society. It was in this environment that Bert Hannam found himself confronting questions about the trustworthiness of the police in the difficult post-war years.

Arguably, the state of society during and after the Second World War was the fundamental cause of the turmoil around police integrity and adherence to rules and regulations. War breaks down normal relations and habits; established procedures are whittled away by the exigencies of extreme demands; short-cuts tend to bypass morality as well as official procedures. Even more important, the work of applying the law becomes more embroiled in survival and pragmatism than in good practice and probity. In short, war sends the moral compass askew. Corruption had been allowed to take hold. The rotten apples were in the barrel. The question was, how does one dispose of them? Better yet, how does one *find* them?

The decade after the end of the war with Germany and Japan brought an uneasy and deprived stasis, when clearing up took precedence and readjustment to normal life was clearly going to take a very long time. Around London, and Bert Hannam's patch, the landscape was one of desolation and devastation: bombed-out buildings and rubble dominated, and poverty was so widespread that crime could only thrive. Atlee's Labour government took over after Churchill's determined and pragmatic fight for survival. The atmosphere of exhaustion mixed uneasily with that of moral imbalance. On the one hand family values in a new era of peace offered glimpses of a return to stability, but on the other hand desperation mixed with opportunistic crime led to social problems.

In 1950 there was particular concern over the issue of juvenile crime, and letters to *The Times* revealed widespread concern. One writer gave some specific information on this: 'These gangs of young roughs, with an average age of perhaps sixteen, appear to be formally organised under such names as The Diamond Gang of Islington or The Brick Gang of Bermondsey, with their own rules of membership and a regular subscription to cover the fines of those who fall into the hands of authority.' In those words we may perhaps see the future rationale of the gangs described in the memoirs of figures such as the Krays, Jack Spot and Frankie Fraser.

The papers were also full of fearful accounts of roughs teaming up as 'cosh gangs', and there was a clamour from some quarters to bring back corporal punishment. Many wanted the birch back in use, and in fact the magistrates' official body took a vote, the result being an overwhelming desire to bring back flogging. But in Parliament the majority opposed this view. It became common knowledge that there were gangs in the cities, but very few would have analysed the situation in criminological terms, searching for a deeper understanding of the phenomenon and considering preventive measures. Consequently, combating crime was solely in the hands of the police force, which was under all kinds of pressure.

In the 1951 report issued by Sir Harold Scott, Commissioner of the Police of the Metropolis, the crisis in police manpower was noted, with *The Times* stating that 'a net loss of 198 men in the first quarter of 1951 underlies the seriousness of the position. About £10,000 was spent on recruiting publicity during the year.'[40]

In this atmosphere, gangland and the mobs dominated much of the criminal scene. The police force was understrength, and if at least some of the oral history of crime bosses is to be believed, there were, as the slang phrase has it, 'bent coppers'. Where there is power there will always be temptation and the possibility of corrupt practices, but in the early to mid-fifties in particular it appeared that the police were becoming anything but trustworthy.

It was in 1954 that a truly newsworthy corruption scandal surfaced, and it involved the underworld of the vice rackets run partly by Maltese immigrants. Throughout the war, Britain's involvement with Malta had led to stronger ties, and consequently to an influx of Maltese immigrants after 1945. Oral history from servicemen in the war often includes tales of local Maltese men 'selling their sister' to sailors for a bar of chocolate, and arguably behind this anecdotal evidence there lies a deeper problem. The island was certainly in serious trouble. Immigration to Britain was not on a massive scale, but over 8,000 Maltese came to Britain between 1963 and 1970; before that there was a steady but moderate rate. Overall, 30 per cent of the whole Maltese population emigrated between 1948 and 1967.

One of these Maltese, a certain Joseph Grech, was the focus of an investigation led by Hannam. In 1954, Grech was charged with a burglary in Lancaster Gate. The value of goods taken was £1,100 – a sum that may be multiplied by thirty to arrive at current values. Grech's partner was Tony Micallef, a big man in the vice business. Grech began to make allegations about the questionable involvement of police officers in the crime. Police thought that a second key was used, as Grech had not had to break into the property, but a strange fact emerged: Grech's own house key was the same as that for the property which was burgled. Grech was given a three-year sentence and sent to HMP Maidstone. From there he began to cause trouble for the police.

Three men were named in Grech's allegations: Ben Canter, a solicitor; Robert Robertson, a detective; and Morris Page, a job buyer. The charges had to be investigated, as the press broadcast the issue. Bert Hannam was called in. After some initial enquiries, Hannam went to Canter, and the press reported it with due drama: 'Superintendent Hannam said that on September 9 he went to Canter's office in Lincoln's Inn Fields and told Canter he had a warrant for his arrest. Canter replied, "It is fantastic and ridiculous." Canter's office was then searched and in his diary for the date September 6, 1954 there appeared an entry: "See Jock Robertson, Willesden." Under the date October 1, 1954, there was another entry: "One o'clock, Robertson, Bow Street."'

By early December 1955, the situation was clear. Bribery and corruption was now being openly investigated. The Commissioner of the Metropolitan Police, Sir John Nott-Bower, made a statement to the press, referring to the completed trial at the Old Bailey in which all three men – Canter, Robertson and Page – were convicted and given custodial sentences, and he explained that after two petitions to the Secretary of State, Hannam had been given the task of leading the enquiries, and that there had been perjury and corruption by two CID officers and three uniformed officers. From Grech's mouth the allegations were only hearsay, but they had led to Hannam's systematic investigation.

The trials ended in November, and Hannam was thanked for his 'patient and excellent enquiry' by Lord Goddard, the Lord Chief Justice. The case of Robertson must have been singularly disappointing for the Met, as his record had been impressive. He had joined the police in 1939, and he had been a flight sergeant with the RAF in the war. He had joined the CID in 1946 and had been given twenty-six commendations. At the trial, when a witness tried to speak up for the detective and offer more complimentary words, Maxwell Turner, prosecuting, said, 'I do not think His Lordship wants to know about that.' There was, understandably, a swell of hatred and contempt for such a failing within the ranks of the police.

What the whole business did do, though, was highlight the operations of vice and police in the areas of London run by the Maltese and other criminals controlling prostitution. At the heart of the very shady business involving Grech and Robertson was the fact that the detective had received a large payment to ensure that the lock on the door of the burgled house would be changed.

Hannam now went even further. The Met had to be seen to be acting after such a disgraceful affair, and Hannam was to lead a large-scale enquiry into police corruption, taking in the whole spectrum of operations defined as vice, from gaming houses to prostitution. Naturally, there would be intense press interest, and sure enough the *Daily Mail* insisted on pumping up the pressure by claiming that Hannam had gathered evidence from at least forty men, revealing widespread corruption. The paper wanted to express as strongly as possible the suspicion that a general system of bribery was in progress, involving payments for favours. This may not be supported in official history, but it is there in the memoirs and biographies of the London gangsters and influential criminals, who generally recall a universal understanding that buying favours was an accepted part of 'oiling the wheels of crime', an operational cost of running a business, albeit one beyond the law. For instance, in *Getting It Straight*, a book in which Freddie Foreman and Tony

Lambrianou talk candidly to Carol Clark, we have a section called 'The Wrong Arm of the Law' in which Foreman says this of the Premier Club in Little Newport Street: 'That was the "in" place many years ago. If ever you had to do a deal with the Old Bill, you know, to part with a bit of the readies and get out of trouble, that was the club you went to. You got the introduction and you'd go over in a corner and sort your business out. It was like a policeman's canteen. Full of coppers in there.'[41]

The printed allegations of widespread corruption led to Christopher Shawcross taking the opportunity to complain to Lord Goddard, as he was defending Canter. The gambit was made because it could have led to the *Mail*'s assets being frozen, with a writ of attachment being issued. But Goddard ruled that there was no link to the case under scrutiny, and Canter wasn't let off the hook.

The lines were drawn for a battle between the *Mail* and the Met. Top legal brains, however, sided with the *Mail* and demanded action. The powerful Police Federation, which had in the past been militantly opposed to high command and the police hierarchy as a whole, now wanted everything cleared up, and a resolution achieved, to satisfy the nation that the police force was trustworthy and above the blandishments of the underground tempters.

As Hannam was pursuing the larger enquiry, something else happened: files from the Criminal Record Office were found in a private flat, with the now vilified Robertson claiming the files had been lost. The man at the centre of that fiasco was DS Thomas Mills, who had not only stolen files but had been involved in assisting in an illegal abortion trade; he had even taken criminal records and Fraud Squad materials. Another police inspector, one Jacobs, fell under scrutiny at this time also; he was dismissed for helping people establish a brothel.

All these events centred on London, but Brighton soon became the focus of its own corruption scandal. The Hannam procedures had nosed further afield. The Chief Constable at Brighton, Charles Ridge, told a meeting at the town hall that Scotland Yard were looking into allegations of corruption. Shortly after that, Ridge himself was arrested, along with other officers, and two of these – Hammersley and Heath – were found guilty and given prison sentences. This affair has since been called 'the plague of rotten cops', and in a feature printed by the Old Police Cells Museum, it becomes clear that the 'good cops' spoke up. The focus of the illegal activities was a place called the Astor Club, run by Roy Bennett. There was also Ernest Waite, who dealt in stolen property. Cash for favours had been the rule, but the 'good cops' had testified. As David Rowland, consultant for the Old Police Cells site concludes, 'It has been said that the public gets the police force it deserves and that the Brighton force was significantly more corrupt than other forces.'[42]

Hannam's enquiries had knocked down dominoes across a far wider area than just London. Historian Donald Thomas sums up the repercussions of Hannam's work with reference to a later event: 'When a Royal Commission on the Police reported in 1962, it made the point that provincial police forces might be harder to control than their Metropolitan counterpart.' Surely this came from, at least in part, the spread of Hannam's investigation into the networks of police power and how these related to criminal organisation.[43]

As we look back at Bert Hannam's role in this episode, it becomes clear that he must have been very highly valued by his superiors in the Yard to have been given such responsibility. The profound issue at stake was in that old adage, *quis custodet custodes?* – Who watches the watchers? To overcome that issue there has to be such a high degree of trust and confidence in the appointed custodian of morals and values that success is assured.

With this in mind, if we reflect on Hallam's ordeal in court in the Whiteway trial, it does appear that his emergence from that proved in some way his status as the kind of detective who could take the lead and be given great responsibility without the slightest hint of any qualms among the top brass, who were beginning to assess his value and express their confidence in practical terms. Little did he know that less than two years later he would face a much more demanding test of his mettle, and yet again he was destined to be in the maelstrom of a court drama that would shake the nation and keep the national press occupied for a long time.

*

After the Towpath case, which had seen him in the role of superintendent, Hannam's experiences tend to confirm a general opinion that he relished 'taking on' barristers and that the courtroom was an arena in which he felt at home – quite able to confront and match the best legal minds in the criminal justice system. He had faced Rawlinson and Humphreys, and both he and his officers had weathered the storm. The modern reader must always bear in mind that these trials were matters of life and death: Whiteway knew that the gallows were waiting for him. Questioning the probity of the police was the desperate counter-attack of the cornered rat, facing the end.

Hannam was acting in a very special role in these conspiracy enquiries. What is significant for us is that he was chosen for them. An examination of his actions immediately confirms that he was the 'lead man' in the team at the Yard when it came to taking on corruption. The objectivity required when one investigates one's own force is awesomely difficult to envisage. The protectors have to be protected, but they also have to be inspected and vetted. Today, all kinds of mechanisms are in place in order to maintain scrutiny on police actions and records; back then, things were different.

It is plain to see that, in the century since Charles Dickens met some London detectives and documented their work, the reliance on 'contacts' and on 'snouts' had remained part of the basic fibre of the profession. How else could an enemy be understood other than by an intelligence system? But such a system brings with it a considerable level of stress for the people enmeshed in the scrutiny of officers under review. The course of the work is delicate, sensitive and liable to generate antagonism and resentment. That is the reason why Hannam was chosen, more than any other: he could cope with the opposition. He could stand firm in the no man's land between the press and the human element in police work. Conspiracy in this context could only be studied, reported on and sorted out by the immersion of someone in the actual material world in which alleged activities occurred.

No man's land was to become a familiar place to Bert Hannam. But his experiences in the thick of controversy taught him a very important lesson: he needed friends and colleagues who could be trusted and who would work in a team the way he wanted. He found such a man in George Lyle during the Towpath investigations. Lyle was one of the first men in the ranks of the Drugs Squad at the Met, and his work included raids on London opium dens; he was later to work in the Blair Peach investigations and also into the deaths of IRA men, including Bobby Sands. Lyle was Hannam's kind of copper, and even more so was Charles Hewett, who figures prominently as Hannam's detective sergeant in the case which was to prove to be the greatest challenge of the Count's career.

7

DID THE DOCTOR DO IT?
1957

Some criminal investigations are capable of comparison with the greatest novels. They have their cast of intriguing characters, they escalate from the mundane to the epic, they draw the reader deeply into an ambiguous world in which good and evil coalesce, and they often provide endless puzzles and riddles, never yielding to logic and reason. Such a case emerged in a cosy seaside town, and the result was a story that perhaps even Dickens or Tolstoy could not have conceived. It was enough to sustain a lifetime of analytic interest, from everyone on the readers' spectrum from true crime aficionados to professors of criminology. It entered the medico-legal canon, as its implications reached out into knotty moral issues. In short, it was a criminal case destined for the record books as well as the popular magazines. And of course, Bert Hannam was fated to be one of the principal characters.

Before entering into an account of one of the most controversial criminal trials and cases of the twentieth century, it will be helpful to establish a tentative normality on which to base enquiries and questions. This could be that of a general practitioner going about his business, or it could be a serial killer's everyday life. Hence the dilemma facing any writer who has approached this singularly puzzling yet fascinating story.

The location is Eastbourne, on the south coast of Britain, a few years after the Second World War. Normality has returned after the intensive bombing of the war years, and those medics who had been called out to give essential help and treatment to those who suffered are now back on the rounds in their normal routine as general practitioners.

One of these doctors was John Bodkin Adams, who had run a practice in the seaside town since 1922. He had borrowed cash from a patient in order to buy his home at Trinity Trees, in a pleasant part of town. Eastbourne was at this time split into two distinctly different communities: the rich to the west of the pier, and the average to the east. Those to the east generally lacked the funds necessary to indulge a doctor in regular call-outs.

As to the wealthy patients, in their mansions, villas and well-landscaped retreats, they needed close attention – and paid well for the privilege. Dr Adams, who came from a respectable Plymouth Brethren family in Northern Ireland, was a familiar sight visiting his rich patients; earlier, his transport around the area had been by bike, then motorbike, and finally by car. He was an ardent lover of fine cars. He also lapped up the high culture of the milieu in which he had ensconced himself: dinners, jaunts, club meetings, lectures, entertainment and so on. He moved in the social circles of the town elite.

Dr Adams was stocky, solid and indeed a presence in every way. He was noticed. Caring for National Health patients was the daily grind for many doctors, but Adams had taken care to gather status as well as qualifications. After starting his career as a junior doctor in Bristol, facing the tough demands of emergency cases in a general hospital, he had acquired a qualification first in public health and later in anaesthetics. The latter had made him especially useful in wartime conditions, when a quick and radical response was often needed 'in the field' as it were.

By the mid-fifties, he had served for thirty years in Eastbourne. One can imagine him arriving at his imposing family residence on the cliffs looking over the sea. It was a rewarding life in many ways: in friendship, of course, but also in a material sense. This is because wealthy patients in such surroundings placed a high premium on the personal attention given them by their family doctor. The long tradition in Britain of having a trustworthy personal family doctor has a strong place in the Bodkin Adams story, as will be seen.

That material wealth came, naturally, in legacies. 'The legacy doctor' was long a familiar figure in social history. What was more natural and proper than the notion that the man who had cared for the deceased, supported them, helped them cope, advised them on every thought and plan, should receive a reward after the patient's death? After all, the doctor was a professional man in a world of wealth, status and material comfort, and in the case of Eastbourne this all took place in a deeply conservative (and Conservative) community.

A doctor who was sociable, personable and wise would be ideal in such a place. Dr John Bodkin Adams looked every inch the solid, dependable doctor, the man you needed when the body started to cramp your style. If a combination of money and medical know-how could add to one's years, then treasure that medico, bring him into the bosom of the family. That was exactly the scenario that Bodkin Adams sought. On top of that, he longed for classy and valuable possessions. He might have been brought up to abjure strong drink and to live a virtuous life, but such principles were long gone. He was very fond of fine wine and good living, and his appearance gave evidence of his being an enthusiastic trencherman.

By the time that suspicions began to be aroused about his possibly easing the passing of some of his wealthy patients, in 1956, Adams had a servant and a chauffeur, and was very far from most people's notions of what the life of a GP is.

The suspicions began with the death of Bobbie Hullett. Adams had been a friend as well as a doctor to the Hulletts, Jack and Bobbie, and Jack died on 14 March 1956. Adams was left £500. Then, when Bobbie died, the doctor had a Rolls-Royce. As Hannam put it in his report, 'We suggested that, on her death-bed, he extracted from her a cheque for £1,000.'

When the famous comedian Leslie Henson rang the police to express his suspicions at the death of his friend Bobbie, the machinery of law began to turn. An investigation was ordered, and so enter Herbert Hannam, now a veteran of many a courtroom combat, to dig into the life and patients of Dr John Bodkin Adams.

A search of death records at Somerset House soon made Hannam realise that there was a mammoth task ahead. He needed a team. Pictures from the press reports of the time show Bert with DS Charles Hewett of the Yard and DI Brynley Pugh of the local constabulary. There was a need to have the right men. Charles Hewett, born in 1914, came from a line of Berkshire Constabulary officers. His career in the police was initiated by a chance meeting with a Flying Squad driver whilst driving a Railton car at Brooklands. A friend, Charles Sparks, sold him on the idea of joining the Met, and according to Charles's son, David, this was 'despite Hewett's father having once warned his son against joining the Met'. Hewett joined in 1938 and at first worked in Hammersmith with T Division, then started his detective work in Ealing. In 1945 he was at Scotland Yard as a detective constable. He was to remain in the CID from then on. Eight years before the Adams enquiry Hewett had been involved in the famous 'Battle of London Airport', and the savage, violent encounter was a tough way to be 'blooded' into the career he had chosen. (For more on this see Appendix 2.)

As well as personnel, Hannam had other issues. For instance, just before the Adams case there had been an innovation, and this is explained by Douglas Browne, showing an awareness of the vulnerability of wealthy folk in the 'sticks':

The result of consultations between the Commissioner [Sir Harold Scott] and the Chief Constable of the counties concerned, this new measure entails police co-operation of a novel kind. Though the Country House squads are in the charge of the Metropolitan detective superintendent, Grade I, who takes his orders from the Assistant Commissioner, they are mixed bodies of Metropolitan and provincial police officers, who work together as a unit...[44]

The irony is potent. The 1954 initiative to protect the homes and goods of the wealthy in the Home Counties was a great innovation, but nobody thought that within two years such depredations on those well-heeled folk would be directed by a wealthy man who was trusted, a man in the bosom of the family, who was not averse to walking off with a few valuables as his patient slept.

But there was to be something in this case that was much more sensational than mere police initiatives. This was the familiar scenario in which a suspect was judged and condemned by the press before a trial had taken place. In France, this was exemplified in the first week of September 1956 when it was made public that Hannam had found hundreds of statements and case studies. The French magazine *Detective* cleverly used a headline to express a familiar tabloid ploy. In small print it had, 'We set out to discover if the doctor John Bodkin

Adams is a fantastic...' and then in large print, 'Killer of Women.' The feature showed 'victims' Gertrude (Bobbie) Hullett and Mrs Morrell, stressing their immense wealth, and then, under a large picture of Hannam in a smart double-breasted suit, the text was, 'The problem for him to find out exactly what condition the bodies of the widows are in, resting in the Eastbourne cemetery.'

Indeed, Bert Hannam felt that exhumations were necessary if more precise evidence was to be required. This was because Hannam and Hewett, with support workers, had been busy gathering statements and medical facts and statistics, and the central issue of the case was beginning to emerge: it was the fine line between 'easing the passing' of someone in pain and terminally ill, and actively ending the lives of people who had made wills and left money and possessions to their friend Dr Adams.

Many volumes have been written on the Bodkin Adams case, and little may be achieved by retelling in exhaustive detail the court transactions here. However, an assessment of Bert Hannam's part in the affair (and the work of Charles Hewett) is long overdue. The overriding image of Hannam in this case is that established by Percy Hoskins in his book *Two Men Were Acquitted*, published in 1984. There is more than a little bias in this, and it also suffers from Hoskins' vanity, advertising his own high status in the Beaverbrook press empire. He is keen to inform the reader that he was the most valuable crime correspondent in the land, trusted by both Beaverbrook and the *Express*, and indeed by the top brass at Scotland Yard.

When it comes to accounting for Hannam's role in the investigations, Hoskins makes the Count's report and the research look like something produced by Stalin's inquisitors monitoring dissidents in the Soviet Union. Even worse, he accuses Hannam of rather underhand machinations in the Towpath case; he does so in a paragraph in which he refers to Edward Pickering, his colleague at the *Express*:

At the end of the night Rawlinson and Edward Pickering would discuss this particular cause célèbre. Rawlinson left Pickering in no doubt of his own opinions of Hannam's methods in obtaining the signed confession. It was not that Hannam was lying, Rawlinson said. It was the method he had adopted to secure the self-damning confession. A piece here and a piece there. A juggling on context. A clever manipulation. Then the collation. At the best, it was an unsavoury method of conducting a police examination.[45]

This is one of the best accounts one might encounter of how a barrister works in an adversarial trial. It describes exactly how such a man as Rawlinson would have worked, and how, in fact, the defence of Bodkin Adams was to work. In the Towpath case, Hannam had simply met the lawyers at their own game, matched them, and won. Rawlinson did not like that. Now here was Hoskins, a stocky, square man with an affection for forthright manly pursuits, developing a friendship with a doctor who had similar tastes, finding a fall guy in Hannam.

The photographs in Hoskins' book make clear the friendship he shared with Adams, and so demolish any thought that the reader might have that here was an impartial book. One image shows Hoskins and Adams on the beach; they could be brothers, with Hoskins smiling as Adams recounts a tale to his reporter friend. Another picture shows Adams playing chess with Hoskins, and the doctor has just checkmated his pal. He raises a fist and grimaces.

Hoskins appears to have considered that he, too, needed to be acquitted. Perhaps the charge he imagined was that he had sided with a man who was being baited, maligned and pilloried. Perhaps this was true, but Adams' failure to recognise his own cupidity and snobbery would have made enemies, murderer or not.

The worst element in Hoskins' book is his account of Hannam's thorough and impressive work in the investigation; he turns this into something negative, as in this comment on Hannam's report:

One evening paper estimated that it would take him three weeks to complete and would run to 50,000 words. It was actually 174 pages long. On 26 October two morning newspapers reported that Supt. Hannam's dossier on the Eastbourne affair had been sent to the Director of Public Prosecutions, the late Sir Theobald Mathew. The dossier was 'nine inches thick'.

Bearing in mind that Adams had been doctoring in the area for thirty years, and that the numbers of patients he dealt with who were wealthy and likely to leave him money ran into several hundred, then that thoroughness was surely necessary. But Hoskins' account of Hannam's work is loaded all the way through. When Hannam asks questions about medical treatment, for instance, this is characterised as 'sinister'.

The process of the law eventually moved towards Adams, and the local detective, DI Pugh, had thirteen charges to read to the suspect. Many of these covered offences such as 'felonious attempts to defraud' and making false representations.

There are wider and deeper considerations, too, before an account of the trial and Hannam's part in it are explored. One factor casting a shadow over everything in the court was the debate on capital punishment, which was very much in the news in 1956. It was suspended in that year, after the impact of Ruth Ellis' execution on 13 July 1955 – the last hanging of a woman in Britain. The suspension of the death penalty had perhaps been coming for some time; a Criminal Justice Act had been passed in 1948, after several decades of increasingly heated discussions on reform with regard to the hanging of teenage offenders and women, and issues of diminished responsibility. Signs were emerging of a more enlightened attitude to the punishments at the severe end of the spectrum of retributive justice. Penal servitude was abolished, whipping was abandoned, and hard labour, linked to penal servitude, was abolished also.

This was all a prelude to revisions which would impinge on the suspension of capital punishment, and in the interim there was the Report of the Royal Commission on Capital Punishment, issued in 1953. Some of its conclusions hint at the general attitude toward hanging in the years before the Bodkin Adams trial. For instance, one conclusion was that 'arguments supporting abolition of capital punishment are well stated and supported by extensive data in two memorandums submitted by the Howard league for Penal Reform', and another was that 'a concise recapitulation of the views held by the British Medical Council, including thought provoking comments pertaining to M'Naghten's Rules [on crime and insanity] are set forth in its memorandum'.[46] These show very clearly that the trial of Bodkin Adams was taking place when the very notion of hanging was being challenged. Here was a general practitioner, standing in the dock, likely to be sentenced to hang if found guilty of murder.

On top of this, there was the nature of his alleged crimes. Since the 1940s there had been a massive shift in the nature of the crimes reported and sensationalised in the media. The typical crimes seen in the press were not at all like Adams' alleged murders of patients in their beds; they were violent and strangely appealing to a general public now inured to grisly crime fiction. As Alyson Brown has summarised, referring to the criminal adventures of the criminals Spark and Goldstein, who were copying Bonnie and Clyde, 'The allure of Spark and Goldstein wasn't solely based around audacious prison breaks. It also sprang from anxiety – anxiety about a rapidly changing world. Spark later claimed that he invented the smash-and-grab robbery. He didn't, but for all that, the couple operated at a time when there was a great deal of concern about the relationship between crime and the motor car.'[47] What this means is that the jury at the Bodkin Adams trial were hearing about something markedly different to the kind of public drama which had occasioned the establishment of the Flying Squad and the Vice Squad. It was domestic. It had the same emotional appeal as the Elizabethan tragedies of the home, in which theatre audiences saw husbands kill wives, rather than the usual fare of great men slaying one another in political and martial conflicts. The accused was a doctor, and in most aspects very like their own.

The fact that the jury and the public were to witness egos clashing in the cut and thrust of the court gambits, and impressive professionals going head to head in intellectual and moral opposition, made matters even more intriguing. The players in the early stages of this drama were professionals – lawyers, doctors, nurses and detectives – and the hearings before magistrates and then in the coroner's court passed by without any sign of what was to come. Nonetheless, seething beneath the dialogue of question and answer was the pride inherent in the public stature of the people involved.

In the midst of all this were Bert Hannam and Charles Hewett. Their every move was to be questioned, and in the interchanges between barristers and witnesses there was an undercurrent of often sly and snide implication regarding the competence of the people involved, lawmen included. At the heart of this was the issue of the accuracy of the notebooks kept by the three nurses, but as far as Hannam was concerned, the real challenge was to be justifying his actions as the man who, on the surface at least, appeared to be convinced of the doctor's guilt.

There has been much discussion regarding the decisions made on which indictments would be applied. Hannam's preparatory work had seen hundreds of case studies assembled on patients of Adams who had died in circumstances comparable to that of the three deaths chosen for the investigation: Bobbie Hullett, Edith Morrell and Julia Bradnum. In one recent work, an extensive list has been provided of all the patients and deaths related to the case, and what strikes the reader in this is that even a cursory glance at the numbers encourages a conclusion that here was a Dr Shipman long before the infamous Todmorden killer. But of course, we have the benefit of hindsight. There was no Shipman when Adams stood in the dock, no precursor in the public mind of any stature which would force a comparison. There was the Rugeley poisoner, Dr William Palmer, and there was the 1898 case of Dr Whitmarsh, who had notoriously been involved in backstreet abortions, but there was no precedent in the popular imagination for the possibility of a local doctor as some kind of embodiment of murder, greed and fiendish transgression, almost to the level of being a creature from some horror story. Perhaps the worst element of the case was that a monster had been walking the streets and visiting the best homes in Eastbourne, and doing so under the guise of normality and routine. What Hannam's thorough research and information-gathering did was make that possibility seem more real, potentially true. Naturally, the most sensational tabloids, like the French magazine mentioned earlier, could stretch credulity by providing the worst scenario to the public – a scene from a nightmare.

Adams could only be charged with one offence at the indictment. At the hearing, Mr Melford Stevenson summarised the evidence regarding the selected prosecution – the murder of Mrs Morrell. The allegation was that Adams had murdered her with the use of heroin and morphine. It was apparent that Mrs Morrell had not been in great pain and therefore the said drugs were to ease and speed her passing rather than deal with sleep-depriving agony. Of course, it was stated that Adams stood to gain a valuable Rolls-Royce car from his patient's death, along with a chest containing a collection of silver valued at almost £300. There had been police interviews with the doctor, and the key one – which happened, as Hannam was to tell the court, by chance – was to prove an important part of the defence's thinking. This was all said before the Eastbourne magistrates, and it is an almost surreal thing to envisage, because Adams was very well known to the people on the bench.

Adams had been kept in Brixton jail since his being charged with murder, and it was early January 1957 when he stood before the magistrates. He replied that he was not guilty of the charges when they were put to him; then the personnel who were to handle the trial at the Old Bailey were gathered: Geoffrey Lawrence QC was to lead the defence, and against him would be the Attorney General, Reginald Manningham-Buller, backed by Mr Melford Stevenson. The presiding judge was Mr Justice Patrick Devlin (who later wrote a book about the case).

The first step in identifying Hannam's participation in this landmark trial has to be the grilling he received over his actions in the initial investigation. Unfortunately for him, there was the supposedly chance meeting with Adams during that period, when Hannam apparently appeared at Kent Lodge, Adams' home, one day. This was subject to scrutiny after a first clash between Lawrence and Hannam over the matter of the detective's notebooks. Hannam insisted that his notebook should not be taken from him and should not be studied if out of his possession. Lawrence addressed this:

Mr Lawrence: 'I am entitled to see the book. It would be a manifest denial of justice if I am not. It is a vital document. But how vital, I do not know.'

Supt. Hannam: 'If it is decided to retain the book in the custody of the court I ask that it should not be examined except in my presence.'

He was about to return the book to his pocket. Mr. Lawrence asked: 'What are you putting that in your pocket for?'

'Sorry Sir,' replied the Superintendent.

'Might I enquire,' asked Mr. Lawrence, silkily, 'What the object is of seeking to prevent the examination of the book except in your presence?'

'I want to see exactly what happens to that book whenever it is examined by anybody connected with the defence. Never before in my experience has a book been retained as an exhibit. On many occasions courts have decided that a book be examined only in my presence.'[48]

Now, here was an instance of an ego clashing with a super-sensitive police officer who had suffered at the hands of a clever barrister in the Whiteway case; in that case the topic of notebooks, written material and so on had led to controversy. There was a certain mistrust of lawyers and court process in Hannam's insistence on keeping the notebook. On top of that, Sergeant Hewett gave a statement asserting that his own notes were merely a duplicate of Hannam's; again, Lawrence sought to hint for the jury that this was a suspicious detail in the police work.

Added to this gambit was the defence's questioning on the meeting of 1 October 1956, when Hannam and Adams met and had a conversation. Hannam wrote a report on this. It happened at 9 p.m. on the above date, and of it Hannam wrote, 'Whilst walking through

Bolton Road in Eastbourne I saw Dr Adams drive his motor car into his garage entrance in Lismore Road at the back of his private house.' Hannam records some crucially important words supposedly spoken by Adams in that meeting. This is the relevant passage from the report:

> The doctor said to me, 'You are finding all these rumours untrue aren't you?' I said to Him, 'I am sorry to say that it is not my experience, Doctor.' He said to me, 'It is strange. I live for my work. I gave a vow to God that I would look after my National poor patients. I am not taking on any more, but I have kept my vow.'[49]

In court, this encounter would come back to haunt Bert Hannam. Clearly, if one contemplates for a minute the circumstances of that dialogue, it surely emerges that there was something purposeful in Hannam being where he was at that time; it being a chance encounter seems unlikely. Lawrence soon saw this and fastened on to it in court. It was introduced into the trial after the powerful interrogation of the three nurses involved, who had been called as prosecution witnesses. Lawrence had already destroyed the notebook and record-keeping the nurses had allegedly kept, and also secured an astounding *coup de grace* in attacking them when he learned of their discussing the case and the record-keeping of medicines administered while on a train after a day in court.

Lawrence knew that this was exactly the right moment to bring up the chance meeting between Hannam and Adams. The important question here, because the issue of cremation certificates was foremost in the medical procedures which could stack against Adams and give a negative picture to the jury of his professional standards, was what Adams said if pressed on this at the stated meeting. Hannam's reply was from his notebook. It reads exactly like that in the record:

The Attorney General asked: 'Did you say anything to him in relation to the cremation certificate?'

I said, 'You have said on it that you were not a beneficiary under the will.'

The accused replied, 'Oh that was not done wickedly. God knows it was not.'[50]

Lawrence took up the 'chance meeting' topic then more thoroughly:

'Do I understand it was what you call an unplanned, *casual* meeting?'

'Oh yes.'

'That means to say that the meeting was not by any design on your part?'

'It does.'

Suavely: 'It was rather a remarkable coincidence for a chance meeting, was it not?'

'I don't think so.'

Acidly: 'There were quite a number of coincidences that fell together, weren't there?'

Obviously, if the jury had reflected for a moment on Hannam's meeting with Adams on that evening, they would have understood that such an event, even if it was planned, was nothing more than part of how a detective works when trying to nose out information. Lawrence cleverly saw that here was a chance to show the jury and the public an example of how intrusive and unfair the police could be on a poor ordinary mortal. This angle on matters entirely omits the detective's need to find all possible ways to obtain information relevant to the case. Adams had proved to be an inscrutable subject in his position as a suspect in a potentially huge murder case. Hannam knew very well that, after reams of paper-based information had been gathered, there was still the fundamental challenge of extracting aspects of the man's personality, to back up original thinking.

We may easily imagine Bert Hannam's confrontation with the enigma of the doctor as he had been described from a distance, as it were. On the surface, here was a man who had a backstory: in the war, Eastbourne had suffered intensive and extensive bomb damage and Adams had come out well from the work he had done. Since then, over the course of the previous twelve years, when the National Health Service had been introduced, he had acquired 'National' patients, as he had told Hannam. But this was selective information, marshalled to make a special plea for him as a good doctor with a social conscience. Other sources reveal a man who cared only for the well-heeled of the town, and whose hunger for wealth was apparent to so many.

In fact, there is an interesting perspective to be had on this matter. In October 1948, just after the beginnings of the NHS, *The Times* reported on a lecture by Dr Stallybrass of Oxford University; he said, in the course of his talk to students, something that would find an echo in the Adams case: 'To the students he suggested that the qualities of a doctor should include the ability to write good English, a sense of humour, and a bedside – or perhaps an office desk – manner that was the outward manifestation of an inner graciousness, humility, understanding and sympathy.'[51]

Those words from Stallybrass contain the heart of the defence case, in one respect. The contrast between 'bedside manner' and 'office desk' manner is very enlightening. It implies that the new national structure, for the masses, offered something rather more official, perfunctory and regulated than the kind of relationship that Adams had exemplified; in his field, what was on offer was personal supervision, special care, individuated treatment and, above all, a friendship which went beyond any professional status in some cases, and in other cases a strange kind of placement of the doctor as almost a family member. Adams had certainly cultivated a relationship with his wealthy patients which saw him accepted as a member of an extended family circle – something reminiscent of the country-house party or 'shoot', at which various professional acquaintances tended to be welcomed into an intimate circle of like-minded people.

This is the right point at which to focus on the trial. A courtroom trial is theoretically a sealed, self-contained unit; something cordoned off from normal life, allowing for the process of law to focus on an alleged transgressor. It has to have professionals to allow its function, and in England it has to include a jury. 'Twelve good men and true' had, since 1921, been an inaccurate definition, for now there were women jurists.

But essentially, at the heart of the adversarial trial, one barrister is pitted against another, one for the defence and one for the prosecution. They are supported by other people, and thus a team is pitted against a team. In the centre sits the judge. But we also have the witnesses, from the laypeople to the professional expert witnesses, and we have the ancillary staff such as clerical personnel.

Yet that is not the whole story, because we need to imagine a concept consisting of three circles. The inner circle is as just described; the second circle, around that, is the assemblage of writers and commentators from the press and other sources; finally, there is the enveloping notion of the broader influences on the trial, which are political, juridical and intellectual. The three elements interact, and influence is universal. A jury member may read about the case, even accidentally; a lawyer may have pressure exerted; any other professional within the criminal justice system may be subject to influence from superiors and peers.

This structure explains much that was to happen in the long trial of Dr Bodkin Adams. First the case for both defence and prosecution must be examined, so we need to look at the lawyers involved. The trial lasted from 18 March to 7 April 1957. In charge, as the presiding judge, was Patrick Devlin, later Baron Devlin. He had graduated from Cambridge, in Law and History, then joined Gray's Inn; when it came to the Adams case he was sure that an indictment on the Morrell death was better than one for Bobbie Hullett, whose death may have been a suicide. This went against Hannam and Hewett's thinking.

For the prosecution, the lead was Reginald Manningham-Buller, who, three years before the trial, had become Attorney-General. He had been a junior minister in Churchill's wartime government; later he became Viscount Dilhorne. In the Adams case, he was to discount the second indictment against Adams – that of Hullett – giving a *nolle prosequi* decision, meaning that there was to be no proceeding towards a further prosecution. The second indictment was thus dropped.

For the defence there was the very talented Geoffrey Lawrence (not to be confused with the John Geoffrey Lawrence who was a judge at the Nuremberg war trials and who became Lord Oaksey). Lawrence was called to the Bar in 1930. One magazine described him as 'a puckish little man with a mind as orderly as a calculating machine'. This could have been equally applied to Bert Hannam, which explains the fascinating confrontation they would have. Lawrence became a King's Counsel in 1950, and by the time of the Adams trial he had wide and varied experience in both criminal and civil law.

Behind the work of the defence was the Medical Defence Union, which had formed in 1885 after one Dr Bradley had been wrongly convicted on a charge of assault on a patient. Since that time it has been prominent, and busy in claims of clinical negligence, fitness to practise and so on. For the Adams case the MDU assigned Charles

Butcher as solicitor, so he worked with Lawrence and others on the defence case at the preparatory stage. An interesting footnote to the case is found in a memoir by Tony Atkinson, who was related to Butcher: 'Dr Adams presented Charles with a ride-on motor-mower. I often wondered what Charles thought while mowing the large lawn at his house. From time to time I asked him whether he thought Bodkin Adams was a murderer. His answer was always, "No Tony. He was found not guilty."'[52]

These were the professionals gathered in court that January, after months of tabloid journalism making Dr Adams' guilt seem inevitable. Many writers had depicted him as a monster whose nemesis was near as the new year began. Percy Hoskins was in no doubt of that situation, and Bert Hannam was equally aware of the detrimental effects of gossip and urban myths. Hoskins wrote: 'At police headquarters it was again emphasised today that the scotching of the rumours must entail a long and searching probe. And although it could eventually be found necessary to exhume one or more persons to allay public suspicion, no justification for such an action has yet been discovered and no such step is contemplated for the immediate future.'[53] He then quotes Hannam's words: 'No encouragement for supporting the local gossip has been given at any press conference held by the police, and one of the local newspapers, under the heading "imperturbable Eastbourne", has referred in scathing terms to the manner in which the rumours have been repeated in certain sections of the press.'[54]

Returning to the three circles and their interacting spheres of influence, the preparation for the trial highlights the workings of the wider, overarching circle of influence – the politics of the judicial process, which is something now very familiar to general readers, after the éclat of the O. J. Simpson and Menendez trials in the United States.

For the defence side, the preparations entailed the work done by the Medical Defence Union and the British Medical Association, and the gathering of defence material by Lawrence and others. For the prosecution, Hannam was involved, being there as part of the gathering at Melford Stevenson's office not long before Christmas 1956, along with Dr Francis Camps, the pathologist, among others, to look at the medical evidence. They had already been informed that the essential expert witnesses had been decided on, and this was going to be an important factor. Regarding the medical material, it was clear to everyone – medical professional or otherwise – that there were potential offences under drugs legislation, and also, more importantly, questions on the topic of euthanasia. A meeting the day after was more attuned to the notion of a murder charge.

This was at Westminster, and was led by the Attorney General, Manningham-Buller, and included Stevenson and also Hannam and Hewett. The other significant attendee was the Director of Public Prosecutions, Sir Theobald Mathew. Born in 1898, Mathew served with the Irish Guards before being called to the Bar in 1921; twenty years later he entered the Home Office and headed the Criminal Division. His biographer made a point which applies interestingly to the Adams case: 'He was fond of opening his lectures with the words, "I direct no one and there's no such thing as a public prosecution" to underline the principle that criminal justice in this country rests basically on the rights and duties of the private individual.'[55]

Pamela Cullen has looked closely at all the archival material relating to the case, and she touches on the views of prominent medical man Dr Ashby, who, along with a Dr Douthwaite, was to be an expert witness. She concludes by quoting Dr Ashby: 'The evidence that the main driving force in Adams' life and actions was to obtain as much money and goods from his patients as possible seems so abundant as to need special detailing.'[56] That is exactly what Hannam had been doing in the build-up to the prosecution, of course.

Cullen also helpfully recounts the various reactions of the experts in this planning stage to other negative aspects of Adams' behaviour with his wealthy patients. For instance, the evidence Hannam had detailed definitely provides a solid block of information about the doctor's theft of goods, taking them out in full view of servants while his patient slept. Cullen writes, 'The "picking up of one or two things from a dead patient's room" indicated to Ashby "a pathological degree of acquisitiveness". But when such circumstances were considered in the light of Dr Adams' "habit of excluding friends, relatives and nurses", there were "strong grounds for concluding that Dr Adams was systematic rather than haphazard in his handling of his patents and their property".'[57]

My metaphor of the three circles must be brought in again here. These preparatory discussions, which took place with Bert Hannam present that December, make it clear that there was an important omission from the subjects handled in these early conversations: the wider social context of doctoring when it came to private patients and home visits. In the 1950s, the doctor-patient relationship regarding the terminally ill was something which generally evaded close scrutiny, often being an intimate and distinctive matter. In oral testimony and anecdotes, evidence suggests that the general practitioner, when it came to serious illness, and to the possibility of treatment with heroin and morphine, often was made fully aware of the patient's will to be helped to die. A death at home could be arranged without the close presence of a doctor, as was the case of my own grandparents in West Yorkshire. Their deaths took place in their living rooms, and caring was done by daughters and a daughter-in-law. After death, they were in their coffins, with the lid open, for farewells to be said. But they were not rich.

When it came to the rich patients, the same notion of dying in one's home was there, but there would be nurses and servants. This is the focal point of the Adams trial, and it involves the nurses who were present during the final moments of Mrs Morrell. The prosecution apparently did not know that these nurses kept notebooks, and the rather desultory and careless nature of this written record was destined to be perhaps *the* decisive element in the undermining of the prosecution by Lawrence.

The other major voice in the preparation of the prosecution was Dr Francis Camps, who had succeeded the great Sir Bernard Spilsbury as Home Office pathologist. Again, Cullen summarises his opinions in this context. She quotes his particular insight: 'I still foresee the difficulty of saying that a doctor is not entitled to employ such drugs as he thinks to relieve symptoms. This does not, of course, mean an overdose. I can see no possible reason for a doctor not to tell nurse what he is giving except a deliberate concealment for some motive.'[58]

A dark shadow over all the initial legal considerations was the effect of the current crisis regarding murder and the noose. As mentioned previously, there had been an interim cessation of executions for almost two years, up to July 1957. The Adams trial occurred in the midst of this process. After decades of debate and argument concerning the varieties of circumstances and victims in a murder prosecution, there was a need for reform, and this came in the Homicide Act 1957, mainly in its ruling that the death penalty would still be applied in a list of specific homicides: murder in the course of a theft; murder while resisting arrest; murder of a working police officer; murder of a prison officer by a prisoner; murder with the use of a firearm or while using explosives. These categories reflected the substance of a long debate that had only intensified since the 1930s, when heated disagreement had taken place in cases of women hanged and teenagers almost hanged but reprieved, in addition to questions about mental health and the proximity of murders to the social issues which had dogged criminal law since the end of the war and its transformative effects on the world of crime.

There was also a stipulation in connection with a person committing a second murder. The lawyers in the Adams case were fully aware that, should Adams be found guilty of the killing of Mrs Morrell, the second indictment, on Mrs Hullett, would almost certainly result in a second murder conviction. Of course, his conviction would have been issued before the new Act was passed, anyway. All these speculations and provisos did nothing but add layers of anxiety and complexity to an already difficult case, which was being placed in the uneasy grey area between clear murder, as commonly observed, and euthanasia.

There was another influence on the revisionary thinking about hanging as well. This was linked to the murder of one PC Edgar in 1948. The killer, a man called Donald Thomas, was tried and convicted, but the judge knew that a death sentence would not be carried out because the Home Secretary, Chuter Ede, had cancelled every death sentence which had been given. Stanley Jackson explains the impact of the case:

This trial hardened public opinion against the abolitionists, but a Royal Commission was set up under the chairmanship of Sir Ernest Gowers. It took four and a half years to produce a massive but inconclusive report after hearing the views of such disparate experts as Albert Pierrepoint and Mr Justice Humphreys ... Although the weight of legal opinion overwhelmingly backed Lord Goddard's blunt statement that 'supreme crime should carry the supreme penalty', no other judge went so far as 'The Chief', who saw no ground for reprieving convicted murderers, even if insane...[59]

That is a survey of the main players in the case, and of attendant issues. In the first four days, the focus was largely on the medical matters linked to the administration and application of the drugs involved in the doctor's work. Hannam did not figure in this first phase of legal interaction. For the jury these days were extremely demanding, as they had to follow the medical explanations on dosages, as well as trying to understand the nature of heroin, morphine, Omnopon, various barbiturates and paraldehyde. The nurses who had been in service during Mrs Morrell's long illness were the focus of attention here, and without repeating all the transactions between lawyers and witnesses, the aim of all this scrutiny and enquiry was to discover how, when and why the drugs were given. Lawrence had done his homework very thoroughly and he made it plain to the court that he was well informed on the nature and workings of the drugs in question.

An interesting sidelight on the subject of Adams' ubiquitous cure-all, opium, is what may be ascertained from the professional advertising and promotion of the time. *The Medical Annual*, for instance, a solid publication created for general practitioners by John Wright of Bristol, contains an account of a drug branded as 'Nepenthe' and the description explains clearly why and when this would be prescribed:

A preparation derived entirely from opium by a process which, whilst eliminating those constituents that give rise to disagreeable after-effects, retains in the fullest degree the unrivalled sleep-producing and pain-allaying properties of the drug. Preparations which make various claims to unique merit are continually being offered to the profession: they often prove exaggerated and ephemeral. The reputation of Nepenthe is based not on our advertisement but on the experience of thousands of practitioners of successive generations.[60]

This makes it clear that it is the standard treatment for extremely serious conditions in which pain is unbearable and enervating. Naturally, the implication is that the drug is helpful for the palliative care of terminally ill patients. The feature on the drug also gives the dose: 'five to forty minims'. Sixty minims would be equal to 4 cc. Adams was also giving the standard dose for paraldehyde, which was 120 minims. There is no doubt that he was offering oblivion. This has the advantage of giving carers and nurses time off from the demands of the seriously ill, and of course it eases the patient's passing in extreme conditions. But the point at issue in court, in the first four days in particular, was the management and control of the administering of this drug.

Lawrence succeeded in showing the jury that this administering and control was shambolic in the case of Mrs Morrell. We can add to this the facts that Adams at this point was not set to receive any legacy wealth and that his nurses and his partner, Dr Harris, had both been involved in the patient's treatment at some point.

By the second phase of the trial, on day six, the police witnesses began to be involved. It has to be stressed that the heart of the defence's enquiries had been the part played by Adams, and the report in the *British Medical Journal* sums up the situation *vis a vis* the final stage of treatment given to Mrs Morell in such a way that the prosecution must have been weakened:

Dr Harris gave evidence. He said he saw Mrs Morrell on June 12, 1949, and on several occasions in May, 1950. Dr Adams, he said, usually instructed one to carry on with whatever treatment he had been giving to the patient, and to the best of Dr Harris' memory he had complied with the instruction. He said he must have increased the morphine and heroin dose on 12 September, 1950 because Mrs Morrell was in an extremely irritable state over Dr Adams being away. Dr Harris agreed that Dr Adams was using the morphine to effect the sedation which was necessary.[61]

All the salient points impacting on the case for the defence are there: first, the regimen created by Adams is entirely his own and almost sacrosanct; second, the patient is highly dependent for general condition on being close to Adams; and finally, the words 'must have', indicating the loose, vague knowledge of doses and treatment times as given by the nurses, who had been mercilessly grilled in court by Lawrence.

Our main concern is with Hannam's part in the trial, and it was after the interplay about the chance meeting with Adams that Lawrence and Hannam really went head to head. Percy Hoskins provides responses and a commentary in his book on the case. The core of the cross-examination involved how Hannam had interviewed the doctor, and this excerpt demonstrates a typical instance of this battle, starting with a question from Lawrence:

'If you were interested in finding out his state of mind or the condition of his knowledge in relation to the certificate [the death certificate] you could have asked him whether he knew in fact that he was not a beneficiary under the will?'

Hannam replied decisively, 'He had just told me he knew *he* was in the will.'

'If you were interested in finding out his state of mind or the condition of his knowledge in relation to the certificate, you could have asked him whether he knew in fact that he wasn't a beneficiary under the will.'

'His state of mind,' Hannam replied with thinly veiled contempt. 'Of course I could have done.'

Nor did Mr Lawrence conceal his distaste for the witness. He went on: 'That would have been a question, the answer to which would have been very helpful at this stage?'

'I don't know.'[62]

Hoskins makes it clear that there was 'infighting' between the two men.

Even more telling with regard to the kind of dramatic mock disgust and shock that Lawrence exhibited are his words to Sergeant Charles Hewett, who was asked about his notes; the fact that his notes were the same as Hannam's, which was common practice, was a chance for Lawrence to imply that this was some kind of malpractice:

'While you were telling my learned friend about the prescriptions, and all the rest of it, when you were giving evidence, you were refreshing your memory all the time from your notebook?'

Sergeant Hewett, who had a notebook open on the desk of the witness-box, replied, 'Not my notebook. The Superintendent's. I didn't write any notes about the conversation.'

Mr Lawrence looked at him as if in utter disbelief. Incredulous, he leaned forward. 'Am I really hearing what you are saying?'

The Sergeant replied abruptly, 'Yes, you are.'[63]

The fact that Hewett had checked and noted things from Hannam's notes was something Lawrence wanted to make into a shocking scandal, some kind of incompetence. He failed. Hewett gave the most suitable and relevant response: 'Mr Hannam said if I disagreed with anything I should tell him.'[64]

From that point, attention was to turn to the testimony of two eminent doctors, the Harley Street men Douthwaite and Ashby. Hannam must have watched their performance in court with a sense of dismay. At the initial meeting of the prosecution, their views had seemed firm and uncompromising; the same sense was surely there in the magistrate's court in Eastbourne. But at the Old Bailey, they each crumbled before Mr Lawrence's questioning. After the nurses' testimony was found to be faulty, with no correlation between what they recalled and what was logged at the time, the jury must have expected something more reliable and assured from two highly respected medical experts. But Lawrence was on top form, first ascertaining from Douthwaite what circumstances justified the administering of both heroin and morphine, with paraldehyde tacked on as well for scrutiny, and finding a certain slackness and uncertainty in this regard; this was followed by Lawrence's discovery of the drugs administered to Mrs Morrell when she had been away in Cheshire to receive treatment. He argued that Adams was merely continuing the same dosage and type of drugs as had been given by a Dr Turner in Cheshire. Having initially offered assured statements about never giving the two drugs together, this became a floating concept, and confusion followed. Dr Ashby was equally unsure and hedged his bets when asked to express opinions.

The *British Medical Journal* explained the situation at the base of Douthwaite's opinion and linked it to something most relevant to the case: 'The patient's normal reaction to the feeling of pleasure referred to was one of dependence on the doctor, who naturally obtained a complete ascendancy over the patient once addiction had occurred.'[65]

The case closed, and the jury now retired to consider their verdict. Hannam and Hewett had been involved in the early stages of the murder investigations, accruing a huge amount of material which was potentially evidence for prosecution. But the lawyers were in charge of the process in the court, and now the jury, directed by Patrick Devlin, met to deliberate. Devlin's words at this juncture are very important. He had a profound influence on the jury, mainly by reminding everyone what was meant in law by 'murder'. His key words were these:

> If the first purpose of medicine, the restoration of health, can no longer be achieved, there is still much for the doctor to do. And he is entitled to do all that is proper and necessary to relieve pain and suffering even if the measures he takes may incidentally shorten life.[66]

He also could not resist a veiled criticism of Hannam:

> It is said in the first place that Superintendent Hannam waylaid – a matter which he much denied – the doctor on the first occasion in order to have this conversation with him. A contrived interview, so to speak. Members of the jury, it would not shock me in the least if he did waylay him. The police have, among their duties, the waylaying of suspected criminals ... If they waylay the wrong man, and in this case it is for you to determine whether that happened or not, it does not seem to me of itself to be a reasonable criticism of their conduct.[67]

Of course, the very use of the word 'waylay' begs a negative reaction.

It didn't take the jury long to decide on a not guilty verdict – a mere forty-five minutes. Then Adams was taken away, in a ruse directed by the *Daily Express* and Percy Hoskins. Hoskins put his own judgement of Bert Hannam in a forthright manner in his book on the case: 'My conviction remains as firm now as it was then, that he allowed zeal to fog his judgement. In view of this I was surprised that Mr Justice Devlin saw nothing to criticize in the role played by the Superintendent.'[68]

The Adams case at this point moves partly into the realm of popular murder stories perpetuated in general cultural writings and oral history, and partly into the world of revisionism, where so many historians and writers have looked again at the case and come to different conclusions. Regarding the popular cultural opinions, this extract from an anonymous poem which circulated at the time of the trial conveys the kind of feelings going around outside official locations:

> In Eastbourne it is healthy
> And the residents are wealthy
> It's a miracle that anybody dies:
> Yet this pearl of English lidos
> Is a slaughter house of widows –
> Their bank rolls are above the normal size.
> If they're lucky in addition
> In their choice of a physician
> And remember him when making out their wills,
> And bequeath their Rolls-Royces
> Then they soon hear angel voices
> And are quickly freed from all their earthly ills.
> If they're nervous or afraid of
> What a heroine is made of
> Their mentality will soon be reconditioned
> So they needn't feel neglected
> They will shortly be injected
> With the heroin in which they are deficient.
> As we witnessed the deceased borne
> From the stately homes of Eastbourne

We are calmed, for it may safely be assumed
That each lady that we bury
In the local cemetery
Will re-surface when the body is exhumed.[69]

The most recent writer on the case, Jane Robins, was interviewed by the *Sunday Express*, and the opinion she offered is well informed, based as it is on exhaustive research:

Over the decades the rumours gathered force. Patients lingered in semi-comatose states for weeks, even months, though they had been in apparently good health before Adams started treating them. Mrs Anne Donnet was hit by a tennis ball in the eye and Adams declared she would not be able to sign cheques so he would take over power of attorney for her. Her friend Else Randall decided to forestall the doctor and helped her give power of attorney to her bank manager instead. Adams was, she said, 'very annoyed' when he found he had been cut out of the picture... no one dared challenge him. Doctors were respected and there was no real proof he was doing anything more than 'easing the passing' of seriously ill patients.[70]

My own perspective on this momentous trial and investigation springs from a realisation that there was a definite dislocation between the legal characters and the police officers from the start. The first hint of this I saw is in the judge's comments in his memoir: 'The police team was constituted in accordance with the pattern approved by the best detective stories. It consisted of the superintendent and his sergeant from New Scotland Yard, Hannam and Hewett, and of the local man, Inspector Pugh of the Eastbourne Borough Constabulary. All three were present at most of the interviews with Adams.'[71] I detect more than a modicum of malfunction here in the manner in which the judiciary perceive the police.

This was a significant murder investigation, with the life of a man in the balance; there was ambivalence from the start in the cohesion of the government and legal personnel who gathered to plan the way forward. Yet, as this comment makes clear, the police presence was treated as something unreal, slightly absurd, and somehow strangely distant from whatever concept of the criminal justice system was in Patrick Devlin's mind. Oddly but significantly, the French magazine quoted earlier, *Detective*, also made the same kind of link to unreality, directly referring to crime fiction in its reportage, heading one section 'Of Fiction and Reality' and adding, 'We have a very large number of police novels, and we are familiar with the torments of conscience of police leaders in Britain.'[72]

I find this a worrying aspect of the whole case. Not only did Percy Hoskins express contempt at Bert Hannam for doing his job well, but here is the presiding judge, beginning his assessment of the police participation in the case, showing a refusal to try to understand what detective work in the context of potential serial killing actually involves. If the judge in such a case is cut off from true understanding, what chance will the legal staff, the witnesses and indeed the jury have of truly coping with the egregious and appalling potential of the case? After all, as a study of Jane Robins' analysis of many of the other patients' case histories shows, Hannam and Hewett were really on to something significant, and this was long before the rise of Dr Harold Shipman.

Looking at Hannam's role in this case, what comes out of the court interaction is a contempt for police testimony. Hannam also had the added burden of the sensational Whiteway case behind him, in which the tabloids had made it seem as though he was deeply involved in corrupt practice. We can see this reporting in this passage from

The News Chronicle referring to Rawlinson's cross-examination of Sergeant Hudson:

> Mr Rawlinson: 'Did Whiteway leave the room at any time?'
> Hudson: 'Yes.'
> Rawlinson: 'You and Superintendent Hannam were alone in that room waiting for Whiteway to return?'
> Hudson: 'Yes, about three or four minutes.'
> Rawlinson: 'You know the suggestion I made to Superintendent Hannam yesterday that the statement had been manufactured by him?'
> Hudson: 'He told me that last night.'
> Rawlinson: 'I am suggesting to you that Superintendent Hannam pushed several pieces of writing paper across the table, telling Whiteway to sign them at various places?'
> Hudson: 'I strenuously deny that.'[73]

This all relates to the attitudes to the police and their appearances in court as held by barristers. Hannam was caught in this kind of situation, with all that 'backstory' playing a part in the examinations.

This is all being summarised because I see the case as being dismissive, and in fact belittling, a massive amount of investigative work which was done by the detectives. After the deaths of Adams and Hannam, out came most of the books on the case, and the targets ready for attack were not there to defend themselves.

Fundamentally, the Adams case was about the perceived difference between murder as it existed in the popular imagination – involving hunts for violent killers – and the kind of homicide which is inferred by the phrase 'easing the passing'. This persists today, arising every time a legal issue emerges from an assisted dying case.

What Bert Hannam and his colleagues had perceived was a man who was greedy in what he consumed and greedy in his lust for wealth and status, and who enjoyed a privileged position in his microcosm of Eastbourne among his private patients, who worshipped him. He loved the sense of ownership, of patients as well as of cars and chests containing precious silver. This was compounded by his need to put on a false front to the world and act the religious, narcissistic elitist. When he had been swept away from the Old Bailey by the *Express* men and sat down in a comfortable room, he was offered drink, and his reply was to refuse it with the words, 'My son, I do not drink.' A bet on a horse was referred to (the horse was called *Not Guilty* and it won) and he said, 'My son, I do not bet.' Here was the member of the Plymouth Brethren, the son of a preacher-man, still acting a role, even an hour after escaping the noose.

It all raises questions – never really approached by most writers on Hannam – as to the nexus, the interchange, or even the dilemma, of a police officer's personal perception of immoral behaviour and actual definable crime. Because there is no doubt that the detectives looking into Adams saw this man riddled with avarice, who was yet loved and demanded by his aged patients. They saw the moral transgressions, and perhaps thought that such a man should have a fall from grace – not necessarily from a scaffold, but at least from esteem and respectability.

One feels that Hannam would have been happy to know that, in his life after the trial, Adams never shook off the obloquy, the stigma; he must have known that across the world, so many people now knew of his ceaseless desire for more wealth, more possessions and more power over others. If we need a factual basis for this, then Roger Wilkes, writing in 2001 about Kent Lodge, Adams' home in Eastbourne, provides one, describing the 'afterlife' of the doctor in his town:

Adams never recovered. He turned Kent Lodge into a fortress. Screwing his elegant sash windows shut and parrying death threats and cranks promising fire bombs by fitting fire extinguishers on every landing ... Adams, a crack shot, had assembled an armoury of sporting guns at Kent Lodge for competition shooting. But he always dreaded the unexpected knock in the night.[74]

A significant footnote to the Kent Lodge story is that Adams borrowed £3,000 from a wealthy benefactor to buy the place back in the 1930s. That was an immense sum then; Roger Wilkes notes that in 2001 the home would sell for 'more than £500,000'.

This had been a case which had singled out for extreme press attention a number of individuals, and of course a series of judgements and conclusions had been stated in the worst back alleys of the media, where those desperate for easy sensation hang out. Bert Hannam must surely never have liked the fact that he was one of those figures in the story who attracted the attention of the reporters and muck-stirrers, but he was equally ready for the combat required against peers and professional equals. It appears that he never spoke about the Adams case, but he did write some letters relating to it. One of the most fascinating aspects of the man is that his written statements have no evidence of any bad blood or enmity to anyone. Even if he did have bad feelings attached to the case, it is to his credit that it never came out into the open.

There is one last comment on this extraordinary case which highlights the way in which Bert Hannam's status as 'the Count' played a major role. This is in the nature of the 'afterlife' of the Adams case, which takes the form of the staggering level of continuing media interest. The string of books on the case – a small library – grows still, and as a narrative is generated and perpetuated, Hannam and Hewett remain somewhat unfairly singled out after political machinations spiked the prosecution before it swung into action. The narrative has taken on mythical proportions because the media have kept the ambiguity of Adams' life and adventures in medicine at the level of a paradigm in serial killing. He was never found guilty of murder, but such is the power of condemnation by the press that his name has joined the ranks of those criminals whose names and lives constantly recur in popular anthologies of true crime.

When the trial ended, it was still not the termination of Hannam's participation in the Adams saga. On 26 July that year, the Count travelled to Lewes Assizes, which had been the scene of the notorious Brighton Trunk Murders trial in 1934, and had also been where famous killers Patrick Mahon, Norman Thorne and John George Haigh faced retribution. Now it was the scene of more mundane matters when Adams' other crimes were tried before Mr Justice Pilcher. Adams had pleaded guilty to fourteen out of sixteen charges, covering his frauds on cremation certificates, prescription offences and others relating to the Dangerous Drugs Act.

Hannam spoke after Melford Stevenson opened proceedings for the prosecution. He pointed out that the doctor owned four cars, and also detailed some more of the wealth which was solidly behind Adams' well-fed body; he noted the balance in his current account when he was arrested, which was over £25,000. His deposit account alone brought him £665 in 1956. He also stated that over the previous decade Adams had received £3,000 per annum from legacies. In modern values we need to multiply these figures by around fifty-five. He was well heeled by any criteria.

The arguments of the defence prevented a prison term being given, and there were points made about Adams' ill health, and how the murder trial and his time in jail during that period from 20 December to 8 April had caused a deterioration in his general health. The judge imposed massive fines totalling £2,400 and said there was a time when he would have been criticised for not sending Adams to jail.

It would perhaps not be pushing the scene too far to suggest that for Bert Hannam there was a sweet satisfaction in the events of that day in Lewes. These were leftover offences, of course, mere footnotes to the greater story, but the day was free of the heated combat of the top barristers, and there was an undercurrent of condemnation running beneath the more mediated press reports. The commentators on the day at Lewes made it clear that Adams still had to face the panel of his professional peers at the British Medical Council, from which august body he was soon to be struck off – though not for long.

*

As a coda to this this famous criminal trial, there is one element which stands on the side of the defence: the recent history of euthanasia as an issue. Throughout the 1930s there had been an ongoing debate on the topic, and this was boosted by the massive press coverage of the 1934 case of Mrs Brownhill, of Harrogate, who had taken the life of her invalid son to end his painful existence. She was tried and condemned for murder, and was to hang, before a campaign began to ask for a pardon. The Labour MP George Lansbury led a successful movement to grant Mrs Brownhill the Home Secretary's pardon. One press report reminded the public that Mrs Brownhill, in Hull prison, was seriously ill and had undergone an operation there, inside the walls.[75]

Then came a very important landmark in the campaign to have euthanasia made legal, prompted by one of the most important medical men of his time. Berkeley Moynihan, who was to become Lord Berkeley Moynihan, with stacks of letters after his name, is without doubt one of the heroes of Leeds, although he is barely known to people of the city today.

Moynihan was born in Malta and his family always had military connections; his father had won the Victoria Cross at the Battle of the Great Redan in the Crimean War, killing five Russians in hand-to-hand fighting, and later served with distinction in the Indian Mutiny. Naturally, young Berkeley went to Sandhurst, but it was not for him; he was cut out to be a doctor, and he started his studies at the Leeds School of Medicine in 1883, graduating in 1887.

He was the most successful British surgeon of the Edwardian period, specialising in surgery on the stomach, gall bladder and intestines. At the time he was learning his profession, the whole abdomen was rarely explored surgically; that was done in extreme emergencies and almost always ended in the death of the patient. But there was more to Moynihan than his medical specialism. He was prominent in the First World War and became in later life a public figure of great authority, speaking before the most respected and high-ranking people in society. He was a sociable, charismatic figure. In his obituary it was said that he was 'a born leader, and he enjoyed the fame, both professional and public, for which he had not long to wait. It became usual for surgeons from all parts of the world to visit Leeds General Infirmary to watch his methods...' Moynihan travelled across the world to learn more about his chosen profession from the experts in their fields; although he was a learned and dedicated man, his attitude to patients and peers was always sensitive and open-minded. The Hippocratic credo that the patient comes first always counted for something with him. He was so impressive and successful that his fame spread far beyond Leeds. He became the first provincial surgeon to be elected to the Royal College of Surgeons. He came to realise that England was not keeping up with developments in surgery elsewhere; he saw also there was no free flow of information with the surgeons and hospitals in other countries. Increased communication had countless benefits for all concerned, and Moynihan's remedy was to found a journal that would act as a focal point for knowledge and research. This became the *British Journal of Surgery*. This saw surgeons joined together in a kind of club, and Moynihan was in his element in clubs and professional gatherings.

In a letter to *The Times* in 1923 Moynihan makes it clear that he is the foremost representative of his profession at the time, writing about the definition and standing of surgery. In the course the letter he expounds on one element in the work which is not often expressed: 'The practice of clinical surgery makes a further heavy demand upon qualities of temperament and of character which are little exercised in the cloistered tranquillity of the laboratory.' That was one side of his work well explained; the other was the issue of what general practising surgeons were achieving in comparison with the 'scientific' achievements of researchers: 'But there are physicians and surgeons whose lives have been spent in the wards and in the operation theatres of our hospitals whose contributions to "scientific" medicine are entitled to rank with this academic work.'[76]

In other words, in later life Moynihan had taken on the role of public educator, distinguished speaker and spokesman. If the press wanted an opinion or a comment on a topical medical issue, they went to Berkeley Moynihan.

For instance, in 1927 he delivered the Hunterian Oration before the Royal College of Surgeons, taking the opportunity to summarise the success story of surgery in Britain, talking about the attitudes previous to the changes brought about by the great Lister. Before then hospitals had been 'Houses of death', he noted. Moynihan always practised Listerian methods, and in this lecture he explained that it was Lister who had made hospital surgery work less dangerous. In the 1930s, said Moynihan, surgeons went to work 'in a frame of mind completely unknown to their ancestors'. He also made pointed in that lecture to a holistic view, stating that surgery could only advance if it learned from and related to such areas of medical knowledge as bacteriology, physics and physiology. He was talented with an epigram, once saying, 'The physiologist too, should stand by the bedside; there are many things he can learn from better from men than from mice.'

In addition to the public speaking, Moynihan wrote a medical bestseller: *Abdominal Operations*. It was typical of the man to have done that, as he was a meticulous writer in everyday practice, leaving detailed notes on cases from the very beginning.

In 1935, the great man led the 'Right to Die' movement. A press report after a speech made to the Voluntary Euthanasia Society went to the heart of the matter:

> The matter has been brewing among individual medical men for a long time, but it has now come to the present head mainly through the efforts of Dr Killick Milliard and Mr. C. J. Boad of Leicester, one of the most brilliant and successful surgeons in England today ... Both are men who possess a high sense of responsibility and are moved by the compassionate regard of sufferers for whom there is no hope and I am proud to be associated with them in this effort...[77]

For a long time in the late 1930s and into the war, papers carried tales of euthanasia in the face of the hard-line law. There were headlines such as 'I helped to end a life' in *The Citizen* in 1937, and then came the attempt to have a law passed making euthanasia legal in certain circumstances. The Lords threw it out. One argument against was put in by the great Lord Horder, who made his name during the Blitz when he organised public health provision in the wasteland of London. He was the king's physician, so he was listened to. During a lecture he gave a typical experience, and this was reported: 'He sometimes said to a patient who pleaded with him to end his life, "Well I think I would do so but for one thing" and when the patient asked what that was he said, "It is very awkward if you change your mind half an hour afterwards." (laughter)'

This background to the central issue in the Adams trial has not been stressed enough. Hannam had to work to the letter of the law; Bodkin Adams, if he was innocent as decided, was working as a professional in a system with a flexible ethos, wavering somewhat from the Hippocratic Oath, and Lord Moynihan had sided with the 'ease the passing' side. As early as 1934, the question was asked in the press: 'Should a doctor kill?' The report told the tale of a patient who had been helped out of life; no punishments had resulted. It was a kind of suicide.[78]

This note on the recent social and ethical history of euthanasia surely helps the modern reader to understand how Bodkin Adams was caught in a dilemma that all general practitioners must have experienced. It does not in any way convincingly shift the criminal charge, but it does shed some light on his actions, if we forget the added dimension of his being a 'legacy doctor'.

Right: Hannam on the prowl in Eastbourne. (*Detective*, 3 September 1956)

Below: The Yard as it looked around 1940. (Author's collection)

Molly Lefebure, a friend of Hannam's during and after the war and author of *Murder on the Home Front*. (Courtesy of Mr Oliver Gerrish)

Right: How the popular magazines promoted the glamour of detective cases. (*Detective Tales*, 1955)

Below: The body of Olive Balchin, the unfortunate victim of the murder claimed by David Ware but attributed to convicted killer Walter Rowland. (Author's collection)

CHERRILL
of the Yard

The Autobiography of
FRED CHERRILL
Ex Chief Superintendent
of the Fingerprint Bureau,
New Scotland Yard

" It can be confidently recommended"
SIR NORMAN BIRKETT

The cover of Fred Cherrill's book on fingerprinting. Cherill was a member of the team around young Bert Hannam in the new work on forensics. (Author's collection)

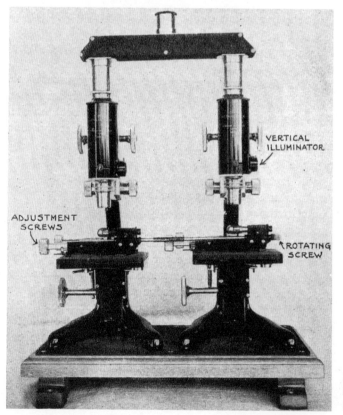

VERTICAL ILLUMINATOR

ADJUSTMENT SCREWS

ROTATING SCREW

Microscopy was coming into vogue at the time alongside fingerprinting.

Right: Press report on the Towpath murders. (*News Chronicle*, 29 October 1953)

Below: Press report on the notebook allegations in the Whiteway trial. (*News Chronicle*, 29 October 1953)

Mr. Peter Rawlinson.

Barbara Songhurst, 16

Alfred Charles Whiteway

Christine Reed, 18

Mr. Christmas Humphreys

Sergeant tells of talk in gaol room

POLICEMAN FAINTS IN

Found axe in police-car, but took it home to chop wood

By GEORGE GLENTON

POLICE-CONSTABLE ARTHUR COSH yesterday identified an axe which is an important exhibit in the towpath murder trial. He admitted finding it and retaining it for 27 days before handing it to his superiors. Then he collapsed in the Old Bailey witness box

The colour gradually drained from his face as he told how he found the axe under the driving seat of a police car in which Albert Charles Whiteway, a 22-year-old Teddington labourer, had travelled as a passenger.

Cosh gripped the rails of the witness-box as he admitted putting it in a locker in the police garage and later taking it home to split firewood.

Mr. Peter Rawlinson — defending Whiteway, who is charged with murdering 16-year-old Barbara Songhurst, who died with her friend, 18-year-old Christine Reed — was questioning Cosh.

Mr. Rawlinson shouted, "Look out," to a court usher as the constable staggered. But for his grip on the handrail Cosh would have fallen. White-faced with his head hanging down he dropped into a chair.

He was given smelling salts and water, and Mr. Justice Hilbery told him: "Put your elbows on your knees and keep your head down as far as you can until you feel the blood returning."

Exhibit 15

P.C. Cosh, who wore the defence and victory medals on his tunic, said that on June 18 he was looking at a police car and noticed the rear offside open. "I went close to it and saw an axe handle."

He was handed Exhibit 15 — the axe the prosecution allege caused the blows to the girls — and he identified it. "I put it in a locker and I went sick from June 23 to July 8," he said. "When I returned on July 8 I went to my locker and the axe was still in it."

Mr. Peter Moore, prosecuting with Mr. Christmas Humphreys: "What did you do with it?"—"I took the axe out and took it home."

Where did you put it at home?—In the tool box in the shed.

Did you there use it?—Yes.

What for?—To chop a few sticks with.

Where did you chop the sticks?—In the shed on a concrete floor.

Did you find any difficulty in chopping the sticks?—No, sir.

When you started chopping the sticks did you notice anything about the sharpness of the axe?—No, sir. I did not notice.

Did it chop the sticks easily?—Oh, yes.

"I saw it"

Did the axe ever strike the concrete floor while you were chopping the sticks?—Yes, it would do.

Did you notice anything about the condition of the axe when you had finished chopping the sticks?—No, sir.

On July 15 did P.C. Oliver say something to you and as a result did you hand him the axe?—Yes.

Mr. Rawlinson: You found the axe on June 18 when you searched the car you were taking over?—I did not search the car, I happened to see it.

Are there any orders given to you for searching cars when you are taking over?—None whatever.

Are there any orders for searching cars after persons have been taken in the car?—No, sir.

A car is just driven away, but in the garage and driven off by another officer next morning. You don't search a car?—No, I did not search the car.

Did you know the driver of that car on the previous day?—I do now, but I did not then.

Did you make any inquiries?—No.

Did you report your find to anybody?—No.

"The practice"

Why did you put it away in your locker and not report it?—The practice among drivers is that anything found in the car is claimed by the driver finding it.

Is that the practice and you don't report it?—I have never found anything before.

Amid laughter, the judge asked: "You are not suggesting that if a man leaves a jemmy in a car the officer claims that?"

"No sir," replied P.C. Cosh.

Mr. Rawlinson: Do you say you were going to keep it for

P.C. ARTHUR COSH
"I chopped wood with axe"

good?—No, but I went sick.

So you take it home because, by July 8, no one had claimed it?—Yes, sir.

At this point P.C. Cosh broke down and it was some minutes before Mr. Rawlinson resumed his cross-examination.

On July 8 you came back from your sick leave and went to your locker?—That is right.

The axe was still there where you had put it on June 18?—Yes.

No inquiries

You had made no inquiries between June 18 and July 8 as to whom it belonged — or

The sensation of PC Cosh collapsing in court after being cross-examined over his treatment of the axe. (*News Chronicle*, 1953)

Mrs Violet van der Elst, campaigner for abolition of the death penalty, creates a problem for the police. (*On the Gallows*, 1937)

Dr Adams as featured in *Detective* magazine in France. (*Detective*, 3 September 1956)

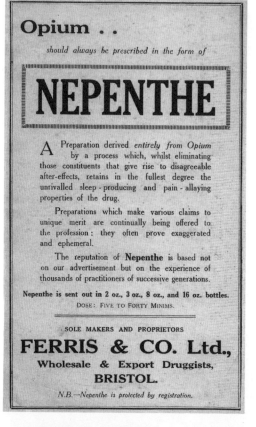

Opium . .

should always be prescribed in the form of

NEPENTHE

A Preparation derived *entirely from Opium* by a process which, whilst eliminating those constituents that give rise to disagreeable after-effects, retains in the fullest degree the unrivalled sleep-producing and pain-allaying properties of the drug.

Preparations which make various claims to unique merit are continually being offered to the profession : they often prove exaggerated and ephemeral.

The reputation of **Nepenthe** is based not on our advertisement but on the experience of thousands of practitioners of successive generations.

Nepenthe is sent out in 2 oz., 3 oz., 8 oz., and 16 oz. bottles.

DOSE : FIVE TO FORTY MINIMS.

SOLE MAKERS AND PROPRIETORS

FERRIS & CO. Ltd.,

Wholesale & Export Druggists, BRISTOL.

N.B.—Nepenthe is protected by registration.

Left: Advertisement for opium in the medical press. Note the guidance on quantities to administer. (*Medical Annual*, 1923)

Below: Dr Adams doing his rounds in Eastbourne. (*Detective*, 3 September 1956)

Above left: Hotel adverts for Eastbourne 1940s – comfort and facilities for the wealthy. (*Ward Locke Guides*, 1940)

Above right: A GP's bill for a private consultation, 1916. Multiply the fee by around sixty for today's values. (Author's collection)

Below: Holywell Mount, home of Mrs Gertrude Hullett, whom Adams was suspected of murdering. (*Detective*, 3 September 1956)

Gertrude Joyce Hullett habitait une merveilleuse maison appelée Holywell Mount, dans le quartier le plus aristocratique d'Eastbourne, dominant la ville et la mer. Pourtant, elle avait perdu sa joie de vivre avec son second mari et ses souvenirs étaient devenus rares.

Above: Adams reading the good news about his trial.

Below: Training school cadets on graduation day, Hendon, 1981. (Courtesy of Stuart Gibbon)

METROPOLITAN POLICE

Tel. :
COLindale 5641

Ref. No..........................

Your Ref..........................

Criminal Investigation Dept.,
Detective Training School,
The Hyde,
Hendon, N.W.9

2/7

Dear Bert,

Many thanks for the loan.

I think your comments on the various pages are well merited. They show clearly the difference between doing the job & commenting on it by what one *reads*

all the best

Tom B

Right: A letter from the training school to Bert Hannam. (Author's collection)

Below: Bert (centre) flanked by son Kenneth (right) and grandson Iain (left). (Courtesy of Mr Iain Hannam)

Above: DS Charles Hewett with assistant. (Courtesy of Mr David Hewett)

Left: A letter from Bert Hannam's son, Kenneth, to Percy Hoskins. Note the restrained anger under the polite tone.

CARSLOWE
BATCHWORTH HILL
RICKMANSWORTH
HERTS. WD3 1JP
RICKMANSWORTH 75891

Mr.P.Hoskins,
c/o Daily Express,
Fleet Street,
London,
EC4   2nd April 1985

Dear Mr.Hoskins,

I am the son of the late Bert Hannam, myself a
retired Commander of the Metropolitan Police.

I have just read your book on the Bodkin Adams case,
and can well understand the need to have delayed
publication until the two chief characters had died.

For all the good it will do my late Father or myself,
I feel I have to make some comment in his defence,
although I know less about the real issues than
probably even you.

I fear my father found disfavour in the eyes of many
of the conventional; he dressed and spoke well and
had enormous pride in the Police service as opposed
to his role in it. His integrity was always beyond
question (although you hint he was a liar), and his
personal standards were such that on retirement,
despite the offers from certain quarters of Fleet
Street, he refused to write or say one word. Ask
yourself how many senior Detective Police officers -
or even parties in the Adams case - refused that
kind of easy money or had those principles.

8

CALLED UP NORTH
1957

A detective in a murder investigation is prepared for the unwholesome work of searches in mud and long grass for material evidence; he is well primed for the interrogations, and he expects more lies than truths, suspecting everything that is said until verification is achieved. He is also prepared for the blood and guts at the crime scene, but when the battered corpse is a frail old lady one suspects that the horror of the scene will generate bad dreams and emotional scars. He or she is arguably never really prepared for that. Such was the shock of this case, in a place of heavy industry, but also a place where family life, religion and the kindness of good Yorkshire folk were all evident, as much woven into the fabric of life as the patterns on Crossley's carpets, the creation of one of the great benefactors and businessmen of the textile town on the Calder.

On 10 June 1957, as Bert Hannam was only just recovering from the stresses and strains of his work on the Adams case, the *Halifax Courier* carried this brief announcement:

SCOTLAND YARD AID IN SHOP MURDER

The Chief Constable of Halifax, Mr. G. F. Goodman, yesterday called in Scotland Yard to investigate the murder on Saturday afternoon of Miss Emily Pye, aged 80, whose body was found in the living room behind her grocery and hardware shop in Gibbet Street, Halifax. She had been killed by blows on the head.[79] Miss Pye, described by neighbours as 'a pleasant old lady' lived alone.

It was going to be a job for the Count of Scotland Yard.

There is a very long history of detectives and other personnel from within the criminal justice system being called out of London to sort out cases in the provinces. Before the professional detective force of 1842, there had been the Bow Street Runners, called out in response to such national emergencies as the Luddites and rioters during the Napoleonic Wars. There had also been some use made of that shadowy body of men the King's Messengers, who acted in a police capacity at times of emergency conditions. But later, once Scotland Yard had its Special Branch and a better-manned detective section, there were plenty of examples of them going out to work in the shires. By the 1950s this was part of the overall concept of their work, rather than a special action. 'Send for the Yard men' was a cry for help that could be heard anywhere in the land.

The strangest and most surprising criminal riddles often necessitated the summoning of the Yard men. For instance, during the years from 1920 to 1923 there was a perplexing case at Littlehampton in which, as one writer summarises, 'Scotland Yard loaned one of their finest officers, George Nicholls, to check that the right culprit had been identified. Hilliard [the author of the book being reviewed] contrasts the woeful inadequacies of West Sussex Police and its young provincial constable assigned to assist Nicholl with the approach of the Metropolitan Police detective.'[80] This gives some insight into the resentment that festered between police forces and the Yard.

Hannam had experienced this potentially eventful clash before, of course, notably in Berkshire, Manchester, Teddington and Eastbourne. Now, close to what would be the end of his police career, he was called to Halifax, West Yorkshire.

Within the previous twenty years there had been many other crimes around the town needing help from the Yard. In 1938 there had been the notorious 'Slasher' case; then in 1943 another charismatic Yard detective, Inspector Greeno, had come north to work on the murder of Mark Turner, who was killed by a Canadian soldier camped on Savile Park (later the scene of a killing by the Yorkshire Ripper). Just before the Emily Pye case, there had been the horrendous murder of six-year-old Mary Hackett in Lister Lane. As the *Halifax Courier* pointed out, 'All the cases were cleared up.' Could Bert Hannam clear up the Emily Pye case?

The Yard detectives perhaps had long memories and were likely aware of the strange 'Slasher' case, which was very rare in criminal history. In November 1938 ordinary folk had been attacked, seemingly by a creature that became known as 'the Halifax Slasher'. The Yard detective who had travelled north back then was Chief Inspector Salisbury, and his thorough investigations resulted in a bizarre conclusion, described in the Quarter Sessions reports and then in the pages of a journal: 'The Slasher was a mythical person and there was no doubt that in all the cases except one the wounds were self-inflicted and that in the one case if such an assault did occur it was done by a person known to the accused.'[81] Thanks to its bizarre nature, the case attained the status of urban myth.

Halifax, then, seldom prominent in the annals of serious crime, had some odd events in its recent history. Only a few years before the Pye murder, there was the horrendous killing of little Mary Hackett, and that took place only a short walk from Emily Pye's shop. The girl's body had been put beneath some flagstones. This, together with the gothic address of Gibbet Street, gave the murder an added resonance in the press, as did the fact that the shopkeeper was eighty years old and just four feet nine inches tall.

On Whitsun Saturday of 1957, Hannam and Detective Sergeant Rowe, both of the Yard, were on their way north to Halifax. They had been called in by the chief constable of the town very soon after the body of Emily Pye was discovered, brutally murdered, in the house behind her grocer's shop on Gibbet Street. Emily had been severely bludgeoned to death in what one officer described as 'a rain of blows to the head' by a ruthless killer.

The town end of Gibbet Street is today in the heart of Halifax's Asian community; there is a mosque quite near to the shop which still stands where Emily's was all those years ago. The streets around are crowded and busy. The thoroughfare of Gibbet Street leads down to the centre of the town and is always noisy. In 1957 it was not so busy, but it is easy to imagine what it was like then, as the red-brick terraces still stand behind the current establishment, and Back Rhodes Street, in which her home stood and where she was killed, is still there, unchanged.

It was a Saturday when Emily died. Police later found that the shop and the house had been locked from around 1.45 p.m. Her body was discovered by her relatives, Derek and Doris Wilson of Northowram, who had come to invite Emily to spend some of the holiday with them; Doris was Emily's niece. But they found the premises locked, and through a window Derek saw the old lady's body, covered with a rug.

The whole investigation was dramatic and high-profile. The forensic specialists came, including Professor Tryhorn from the Science Laboratory in Harrogate. Crowds gathered to watch as officers stood around talking, or walked through enclosed alleys, before action was taken. It was a senseless murder, apparently done for a small amount of money taken from the till. It became clear that another, more substantial amount of money was hidden on the premises and had not been found. Superintendent Hannam said he would not have been able to find it. The murder was possibly not done by anyone who knew her, then, and police at the time thought that it may have been an opportunistic killing by a passing customer, perhaps en route to Lancashire.

It was unusual for a high-ranking officer such as Hannam to be there. He was noted to be a smart, dapper man, wearing a Homburg and a very expensive suit. A picture in the local *Halifax Courier* shows him almost posing for the camera, looking dignified and impressive. He was forty-seven by now.

Emily had been a popular and warm-hearted person, and had lived alone for fifteen years, but before that she had had a 'life-long companion' for thirty years – as long as she had owned the business. At one time, when she had been ill and had closed the shop, Emily had told her niece that she thought a lot of the customers and ran the shop more as a hobby than anything else. All the more horrible, then, that such a kind and sociable woman should die in that way.

Considerable force was used to kill Emily; it had all the hallmarks of a violent robbery, and was representative of a type of killing observed everywhere. In the early to mid-1950s there had been a stream of such attacks on lonely women living alone, often on commercial premises. The ultimate irony is that the plain, low-key figure of Emily Pye attracted in her death a media frenzy and a host of law officers who became local celebrities overnight. Such detail was given about Herbert Hannam that readers of the local papers were told that he wore 'designer' clothes and the information was offered that his son was highly educated. Hannam was interviewed almost as if he were a figure from a *Boy's Own* feature; much was made of his involvement in monetary fraud investigations in the USA. He was, undoubtedly, a remarkably interesting figure to find walking around a northern industrial town.

One of the most thorough reports in the local press gave a full picture of the investigation. Hannam was interviewed and made his work clear to the press: 'The Scotland Yard chief … made a special appeal to Halifax people for information about anyone who was not at home between 12 noon and 3 p.m. on Saturday. "I know this sounds an enormous task, but I would like to see them, all the same." This was a most terrible crime. This woman was really brutally attacked.'[82]

The same report gave a more comprehensive picture of developments:

Intense police activity developed in and about the house this morning with the arrival of Supt. Hannam, who was accompanied by DIC C. Payne of the Halifax CID and Prof. F. G. Tryhorn of the North Eastern Area Forensic Science Laboratory. Hannam and Payne spent some time inspecting the yard just outside the premises … the two police officers walked along Back Rhodes Street to an entry leading to Hampden Place.[83]

There was then a massive house-to-house enquiry across a very wide area. Hannam was obviously keen to hear from anyone who went into the little shop on that fateful day, and questions were asked of taxi drivers and people at the railway and bus stations.

But nothing came of the enquiry, and it remained unsolved until a deathbed confession given to Calderdale police in 1988, the full details of which have not been released. Superintendent John Parker told *The*

Halifax Courier: 'This man made a number of anonymous calls. He told the newspaper that his father had admitted to Emily's murder two or three days before he had died. The caller refused to give details because his mother was still alive at the time and unaware of her husband's secret.' The man added that his father had said what he had done was not worth the anguish he had gone through. In 2006 police again appealed for the caller to come forward with full details, but as yet there is no closure.

Hannam and Rowe had come north, been highly visible, attracted the media, and then returned home empty-handed.

Since that investigation, there have been a series of appeals to the public, as the cold case continues to be gather attention. In 2007, for instance, the *Yorkshire Evening Post* carried a feature: 'Do YOU know the killer of Gibbet Street?' The article gave powerful details, such as how 'her killer robbed the till and escaped through the back door ... but before fleeing he locked the front door and covered her body with cushions, towels and a pile of paper ... to prevent anyone looking through the window and spotting her body'.[84]

Also at that time, thanks to the efforts of David Glover, who wrote to the *Halifax Courier*, readers learned more about the little woman's life. She was born in West Bromwich in 1876, one of four daughters of a furnaceman in a glass factory. David Glover wrote, 'By the time of the 1891 census, Emily was working as a servant in the Victoria Arms, a pub in Pellon.' The landlord's widowed sister, Matilda, became a close friend of Emily, and David adds, 'It was in 1928 that she took over the corner shop at 123, Gibbet Street where she was to die. Initially she shared the premises with her friends John and Matilda Harwood. Matilda died in 1938 and John in 1944. After this, Emily lived alone.'[85]

I have a relevant coda to the story. In 2003, when my book on Halifax crime was published, I was giving a signing in a Halifax bookshop. From the corner of my eye, I saw a woman standing rather nervously by the counter, but I had a line of people wanting to talk to me, so I could not speak with her. When the signing ended, the manager of the shop told me that the woman had wanted to see me and talk about the Pye case, but she had had to go. All that could be said was that the person had been a bank teller and knew Emily. Apparently the old lady always took bags of coins to the bank. We know that she kept most cash in the back room, but the killer never found it. All he took was £6 from the till.

*

Sadly, then, Bert Hannam did not leave Halifax with the case cleared up. Even the new-fangled police dogs from Wakefield had not revealed anything significant. (In 1954 a Home Office Working Party Committee had looked at the co-ordination of training and breeding the dogs.[86]) It was to be the last major case in Hannam's police career. It must have been hard to travel back to London knowing the killer was still at large.

There are some crimes which are so disgusting and outrageous that officers of the law cannot possibly avoid being affected by them, and this was one such case. A tiny, defenceless and harmless old lady had been brutally killed on her own premises. The killer 'needs' to be identified, urgently. Hannam must have felt a keener sense of failure than he usually would have in such a situation. Even today, we still await some kind of resolution of this horrendous tale of senseless, revolting murder.

It has to be stressed that the 1988 deathbed confession raises the question of what such an act would serve to achieve, given that no closure for relatives comes from such an open-ended and rather tormenting half-fact. Within my own life experience (I have lived and worked in Halifax), I have encountered the name 'Emily Pye' as something that resonates in the popular memory. Her name is passed on, the sad story recounted; it seems highly likely that this will never change.

It would be quite an understatement to call the case an irritating loose end, an unfinished task; it would be more appropriate to note the widespread frustration at the lack of retribution and the shameful freedom of the perpetrator. The fate of Emily Pye entered regional chronicles of unsolved murders, but it also showed, annoyingly, that sometimes even Scotland Yard could not track down a killer. The appeals for information will go on, and there will have to be the desperate belief that someone, somewhere, has passed down a family history, some little detail about that Saturday when one of the most brutal murders took place in a West Riding mill town.

9

THE MAN HIMSELF AND IN
POLICE HISTORY

Hannam, joining the police in 1927, arrived at a time of severe and widespread problems in the force, largely stemming from a general discontent with professional conditions of service. This was just four years before Lord Trenchard was to take over as Police Commissioner, and before the chief's reforms kicked in. Comments on the overall criminal situation in the capital at the time saw it likened to the Chicago ganglands and bandit country.

In the midst of agitation and discussion, at a time when a police union was illegally in existence, a sergeant named George Miles, a representative of the discontented officers, said, 'Nowadays a policeman must be brave as a lion, as patient as Job, as wise as Solomon, as cunning as a fox, have the manners of a Chesterfield, the optimism of Mark Tapley, must be learned in criminal law and local by-laws, must be of strong moral character, be able to resist all temptations, be prepared to act as a doctor, a terror to evil-doers, a friend and counsellor to all classes of the community, and a walking encyclopaedia.' This was said in 1919 when the Desborough Committee, which was destined to influence the most advanced legislation on police work since Peel's

Acts, considered matters in the aftermath of two widespread and acrimonious strikes.[87]

The heart of the problem was that it was simply unacceptable for the British police force to have a union. The ideology of both civic defence and social and individual security ran counter to such a concept. But the fact remains that at the beginning of the First World War, in 1914, the lot of the police constable was desperate; some were on the poverty line and many were having to do part-time work (against regulations) to feed their families. Although the matter of police pensions had been resolved, and despite the fact that police officers had a day off every week, the constable's income was inadequate to meet the rising costs of living; when the war with Germany developed, all this was exacerbated. Some policemen had to watch their children earning more than them in munitions factories, and one man said that he was in such a bad way that he had to do gardening on the side to survive.

Deeply entrenched in the growing grievances was the rule of 'no conferring': policemen were not supposed to engage in discussion with regard to conditions of service nor to complain. This sense of isolation in the ranks, a sense that nothing could be talked about and that all discipline should be accepted without dialogue, was to create the circumstances that nurtured the leader of the first union agitation: John Syme. He had been involved in a case in which he defended two constables in his division and was reprimanded for his care. He did not take that lying down, and the argument ended with his first being transferred and then sacked. Syme was a meticulous man, and early in his career he had been arguably a 'barrack room lawyer' because he knew the regulations and related legislation on police work very well. The man he confronted and who sacked him was Sir Edward Henry, a former Inspector-General of the Bengal Police who was Commissioner of the Metropolitan force at this time.

Syme met the editor of the *Police Review*, John Kempster, and an alliance was formed that was to lead to the clandestine first phase of what would become two police strikes – in 1918 and in 1919. By the criminal law codification these acts were mutinous, and of course some happened when Britain was at war, so the repercussions were profound for a nation whose manpower was being sapped over in the trenches of the Western Front. Nott-Bower, the City Commissioner, lost a son in that war, and he was certainly in no mood to consider compromise when his men joined in the first strike. It was a case of Syme's personal grievance becoming a catalyst to bring out the other grudges brooding in the force, long-standing and often rankling under the enforced discipline of daily work.

The *Police Review* had been in existence for many years, and one of its functions was to give some kind of outlet for complaints about police work; constables could write, anonymously, to the editor, and their letters would be printed, thus airing certain disgruntled viewpoints and offering at least one way of expressing these things. The journal was popular for other reasons – it was a voice of the profession and it carried informative features. But when Syme met Kempster and other men were gathered around, notably J. R. Penfold and Mackenzie Bell (a Liberal politician), the notion of a union gained strength and support. There was some support in Parliament, despite the deeply held notions of police exceptionalism in respect to unionisation: Ramsay MacDonald in 1907 and Philip Snowden in 1914 had both spoken in Westminster in support of the idea.

When it came to the dismissal of a policeman for being involved in the forbidden union (then known as the National Union of Police and Prison Officers), the inevitable happened and there was a call to strike. The numbers of officers in the union was over 4,000 – a number grossly underestimated by the top brass in the police at the time. In fact, there was a certain complacency and inaction on the part of the leaders; they thought of John Syme as a crank who occasionally irritated them, and probably never thought that he would achieve anything. When Syme was imprisoned in Wormwood Scrubs for libel, it must have seemed as though the strike would never happen; but a few months after the appointment of a new Home Secretary, Sir George Cave, and in spite of a plan to have the widows of dead officers receive a 10s weekly payment, the trigger to strike occurred. It was the case of PC Tommy Thiel. Very popular in the force, Thiel believed in the union and had been encouraging union growth in Manchester. He had been reprimanded for doing so, and was called to Scotland Yard to face the music; there he was dismissed from the force.

James Marston addressed a meeting at the Pimlico Mission Hall and stressed that the time for discussion was long past. A strike was called to begin at midnight on 29 August 1918. Headquarters were set up in Cadogan Place and matters progressed. Troops were called out to guard important locations and issues such as the use of Special Constables emerged, but it was decided that such a move would incite possibly uncontainable confrontation and so it was not followed up, though there were nonetheless isolated incidents.

Within days, Marston talked to a mass meeting at Tower Hill and announced that the City Police were joining the strike. That meant that 6,000 policemen were on strike. The City force at the time numbered 1,200 men; Nott-Bower was actually on holiday when the chief office was given the news that the City men were joining their Metropolitan colleagues. It was the Assistant Commissioner, Captain Bremner, who learned of the news, and his reaction was to go immediately to the Yard and confer with the police there on what was really going on; there was a general disbelief that such a thing would actually happen. Beneath all the drama there was the belief that the 'English bobby' did not do such a thing; it was considered European or certainly 'un-English'. It was the kind of outrage one might expect in the colonies, but not in the streets around the Bank of England and the Guildhall.

Bremner received a telegram that evening after his visit to the Yard for advice. It read: 'Please take notice that same conditions affecting Met. Police will automatically affect City Police. E. C. NUPPO.' He did the right thing and sent the message on to the Commissioner, and then later sent a brief but useful statement to his chief: 'All quiet with us but serious with others.' But that was unduly optimistic, and Bremner had no idea that shortly after his message was sent a City constable walked off his beat and that some men who were not on duty were assembling at Bishopsgate police station; their statement was that they would stay out until told otherwise by their 'union'. Bremner again did the sensible thing, sending the man he thought was right for the task to speak with them before matters got out of hand. The man who went was Superintendent Halford, and he faced an increasingly large crowd. His argument that the City officers were better off than their Metropolitan colleagues had a good effect, particularly when he moved on to the well-tried method of referring to a supposed 'review of pay'. He promised that City officers would have whatever pay the Metropolitan men received when things had hopefully been resolved.

Halford talked about his authority to speak coming from no less a person than the Chairman of the Police Committee at the Guildhall. He had a notable effect, because men returned to their beats, heartened for the time being with a promise that Nott-Bower would receive a deputation in the near future. But the mollification was short-lived. The next telegram sent to the Commissioner abroad was, 'Position critical. Advise your return.' Marston had whipped up the Metropolitan men to move into the City in large numbers, with the clear intention of pushing the City men into joining the strike. According to the historians Gerald Reynolds and Anthony Judge, the City men were 'in some cases bullied' into acquiescence.

After a month of the strike, the issue of the City Specials moved to centre stage; it is significant that they felt similar pressures but, as one anonymous correspondent to *The Times* wrote in September, had other complaints:

> Unlike their confreres in the metropolitan areas, who live close to their homes, City specials have to provide meals entirely at their own expense, which, together with travelling expenses, means a considerable outlay in the course of a year … During the last four years the authorities have supplied one uniform, including an overcoat, one pair of boots and fifteen shillings towards a second pair, the latter allowance being quite inadequate … such parsimony seems incredible when associated with the greatest City in the world.[88]

The writer adds that there was no ill-feeling between specials and regular policemen, so there was some consolation for the authorities, but again this pinpoints a fundamental weakness in the attitude of those in power at the Guildhall and beyond.

The idea of the police union being recognised was a complete anathema. But Prime Minister Lloyd George agreed to meet with representatives, and various groups gathered at important locations so that their discontent was visible for all to see as they went about their business. The City officers assembled by the Royal Exchange, and then a large group began the walk to Whitehall, but only after being reminded that they were 'gentlemen'. It was during this phase of the strike that the future writer C. H. Rolph becomes an interesting source. He was standing by his father, the resolute Chief Inspector Hewitt, when the striking constables walked along Clack Lane. Rolph wrote that the 'gentlemen' did indeed raise their hats as they passed. But what was happening was naturally a high-level threat to security, and in time of war, so Whitehall was now in the hands of troops.

Lloyd George and his advisers knew that they would have to offer a pay rise and put Tommy Thiel back on the beat, and the Prime Minister's words to the representatives as they left, content that most demands were met, were, 'Now don't you forget, if ever a similar situation arises in the future, you may come to see me.' The union issue was avoided, but with a full awareness that there would have to be some kind of organisation in the future which would act as some kind of representative professional body for the police.[89]

On 1 March 1919 the Desborough Committee was appointed to review police pay and conditions; their work was done in two months. This was to lead to a situation in which the concept of a police union was more visibly a central issue – at least for some. This was because the Desborough Committee recommended a pay rise, raising the constable's weekly pay by £2. The Police Federation was also to be established, and the relevant bill went through Parliament and was law by 17 August. The paradox was that the second police strike was called on 31 July, as this was all in motion. It was about the union, its recognition and existence. In spite of the pay rise and the compromise of the Police Federation, over 2,000 Metropolitan men went out – although they were joined by just fifty-seven men from the City. With City support for the second strike so meagre it was mooted that the City police would 'not forget the important duties which they owe to the state, the citizens and to themselves'. It was the expected mix of sympathy and moral plea. Even Christabel Pankhurst spoke up in favour of the police, saying in a speech at Caxton Hall at the same time as the Mayor's letter was being read that she was 'in entire sympathy with the police in so far as they received small pay while they were expected to have the wisdom of Solomon and display a knowledge that would not disgrace a judge'.

The number of strikers indicated a very low response to the call. The most notable disruptions and confrontations took place in Liverpool, where almost half of the total force of 2,100 were out. The strikers were reminded by the Home Secretary that their actions represented a mutiny. No compromise was possible, and what happened was that all the strikers were sacked and none of them were reinstated. The government victory was due to a rapid recruitment campaign and a massive response; a school of instruction was created at Westminster and more than 1,500 recruits came forward.

Marston still pressed on with the die-hards, and reports of his meetings at Tower Hill gradually became more perfunctory as the newsworthiness subsided. There was a certain amount of aggression between the strikers and special constables, of course, and even on their march, done in orderly fashion, *The Times* reported that some strikers had 'molested' some specials in the course of the march, though what this means is unclear. The public were reminded that in the standard policeman's oath, taken on his joining the force, was the statement, 'I will truly declare and affirm that I will well and truly serve our Sovereign Lord the King ... and in all respects to the best of my skill and knowledge discharge the duties of the said office faithfully according to the law.'

Nott-Bower then accepted and instated the new pay scale for the City men; it was approved at the Court of Common Council on 28 July. The commissioner took the opportunity to tell the press that 'the present members of the City force ... may well feel proud of the steadfast manner in which they are discharging their duties during the present crisis'. As a former leader of the police in Liverpool, he must have been looking northwards and feeling relieved that he was then in London, and not on Merseyside.

The achievements of the Desborough Committee were very significant; their measures had remedied the constables' main grievances, and it was simply the union issue that had limited matters in the final legislation. As one MP said, the report 'offered what amounted to a new conception of the police as a service, an integrated system, rather than a collection of separate forces each concerned with its merely local requirements and personnel'.

The Police Federation was also a product of the committee, and the Police Act of 1919 defined the purpose of the Police Federation as 'to enable members of the police forces in England and Wales to consider and to bring to the notice of police authorities and the Secretary of State all matters affecting their welfare and efficiency'.

After all this strife and open confrontation, things had settled down in the early twenties. Nonetheless, Hannam would have been well aware of the discontentment and the aftermath of the troubles. Peel House, where he started training, was formed in the First World War and the general chatter and talk about 'the bad old days' would have filtered through to him.

*

What about Hannam himself, beneath the public image of the smart, efficient detective? This is not an easy question to answer, as Bert himself never bothered about such topics, being apparently content to live a quiet life of domesticity, enjoying family life after his work. Some elements will remain a mystery, but fragments have emerged after my calls for memories and reflections on him. Every writer wants to offer an interpretation of the character of the person they have tried to bring to life on the pages, perhaps lifting them out of that one-dimensional place.

Writers often have to search for metaphors to explain their difficulties in approaching their subjects, and in the case of Hannam this can be likened to a doll's house; if one imagines Hannam's life as such a creation, with rooms for every phase and element in his life, then writing on him is like shining a torch into one little room at a time, only to find that he is there in the shadows, in a corner perhaps, well away from the beam of light. The reason that the man himself is so elusive is that in the public eye he is comprised solely of his cases; he refused press interviews and never courted media attention. This neglect of the limelight is one reason why he is a subject of fascination to his biographer. There is, of course, a large press portfolio on him, but the material there consists of external, distant, somehow distorted and very limited substance.

Nevertheless, the question has still to be asked: what do we know of the man himself? Clearly, as conversations with his grandson and evidence in print from his son confirm, he was well liked, respected and welcomed. After his time in the police he retired into a very different life, much of which went unrecorded.

Hannam was born in Paddington in 1908, and it was generally at that time a well-to-do area. In the great poverty survey undertaken by Charles Booth, published in 1889, the area covering the recreation ground, Lauderdale Road and the stretch from Maida Vale to Malvern Road were categorised in Booth's colour-coding as 'Fairly comfortable', 'Middle class-well-to-do' or 'Upper-middle class, wealthy'. Of course, the area was densely populated, with about 140,000 people living within Paddington around 1910. The station and the Metropolitan Railway ancillary establishments added to the sharp contrast between streets of respectable homes and the industrial base. One survey, published in 1932, explains the larger picture of what would been around young Hannam: 'In 1915, the Baker Street and Waterloo Railway was extended to Paddington, Maida Vale, and Kilburn, this providing direct communication between Paddington Station and Piccadilly Circus. Today the people of London make nearly 4,000 million journeys by train, omnibus and tram in the course of a year, or an average of 500 journeys per head for each member of the population.'[90]

We then need to imagine Hannam's first few months of police work, learning by observation, and studying at Peel House; most of his time would be spent watching closely how others did things. There would be the constant demands made on him to absorb correct procedure, following the right kinds of deferment to seniors, being respectful, holding back what instinct might urge but protocol forbade. He would have been on the receiving end of orders barked out, military style, and would have known what a dressing-down was. Then, as now, pride in the uniform and regalia, the right way to behave and other professional diktats, would be uppermost.

Around the time of Hannam's first year in the force, 1927, the education of police recruits was up for discussion. The Chief Constable of Dunfermline, for instance, lectured the Police Mutual Improvement Association, and he listed a several functions of the organisation, but mainly the aim was to help recruits cope in the difficult world of social intercourse, as it was called then, with peers and public. In Scotland, another chief constable, John Morren, went so far as to write 'a brief, businesslike book, a trustworthy guide to the new problems with which they [young officers] are called upon to deal'.[91]

Hannam's mainline trajectory as a professional detective saw one case follow another, and there was little time for him to reflect and gather thoughts on whatever case had just passed. Such is the nature of police work. There is always sleep to be caught up with, as the last case gradually fades and the new ones comes along, with fresh tasks and lines of thought.

A local reporter in the Emily Pye case interviewed Hannam, or asked questions about him, and gave this profile: 'Detective Superintendent Hannam has been described as one of Scotland Yard's best-dressed detectives. With his graying hair, carefully pressed suit and Homburg hat he looks more like a stockbroker than a criminal investigator ... A man with wide financial knowledge and a grasp of several languages, one of his tasks involved a trip to the U.S. in 1947 to inquire into the illegal transfer of capital.' Once again we have the emphasis on his appearance, and the writer had scanned available material for other details. The world always seemed to want to see him as 'the Count of Scotland Yard'.

It might be useful to quote some opinions in print. First there is Jane Robins: 'Detective Superintendent Hannam was a Londoner born and bred. He was accustomed to breathing a different sort of air, gritty with exhaust fumes or thick with soot ... Photographs of Hannam record a don't-mess-with-me swagger in his walk and a jut to his chin. They show a solid block of a man...'[92] Then there is Pamela Cullen's comment, which places him in a different light: 'He was an exceptionally intelligent and innovative detective and he was personable enough to be acceptable to Eastbourne society, yet not someone to be overawed by anybody or deterred by status.'[93]

A glimpse into his nature comes from David Hewett, son of Charles, the trusty sergeant who worked with Bert in Eastbourne. David recalls being taken to Scotland Yard by his father one weekend when there was paperwork to be done, and Charles was using a duplicating machine for some copying. Charles said brought him over, and there was Bert, 'a charming man' – charming even to a kid when there was nothing going on except the routine grind of a police officer's life when the clerical duties press hard.

David Hewett downplays his father's role in the Adams case, saying he was Bert's 'bag carrier', but whatever else their relationship was, it was jocular and easy. David writes,

> Bert and Charles were returning to Eastbourne Police Station in the afternoon of a day in late autumn, 1956. They entered via the rear yard gate, and as they walked across the cobbled courtyard they noticed the chief constable, Richard Walker, in full dress uniform, being photographed on a police horse [for the force Christmas card it transpired]. Relationships between the officers were very difficult. Walker's wife was a patient of Bodkin Adams and the Chief had only agreed to call in the Yard after prolonged and intense pressure from the DPP and the Home Secretary. As Bert and Charles got nearer to the horse it raised its tail and did a huge dump on the cobbles. Walker allegedly turned to say to Hannam, 'There you are Hannam, that's what my horse thinks of the Met!' Unfazed, Bert looked up at Walker, down at the steaming ordure and back at Walker before saying, 'Just as well you spoke Sir. I thought you'd fallen off and I was going to lend Hewett a hand getting you back in the saddle.'

This may be true, or it may be apocryphal, but as an anecdote it pinpoints the stresses and strains between the local force and the Yard – a factor in Hannam's work which was always a cause of drama and tension.

As noted in the introduction, Bert Hannam did not write a memoir. A man who had faced so many accusations regarding his professional work could easily have responded with newspaper features or even books in order to defend his life's work as he reached retirement. But he did no such thing, and that fact attracts considerable respect. His son, Kenneth, who reached the status of commander (the youngest ever to do so at that time), provided a statement along these lines in a letter to Percy Hoskins in 1985 after Bert's death. This is the text:

I am the son of the late Bert Hannam, myself a retired Commander of the Metropolitan Police.

I have just read your book on the Bodkin Adams case, and can well understand the need to have delayed publication until the two chief characters had died. For all the good it will do my late Father or myself, I feel I have to make some comment in his defence, although I know less about the real issues than probably even you. I fear my father found disfavour in the eyes of many of the conventional; he dressed and spoke well and had enormous pride in the police service as opposed to his role in it. His integrity was always beyond question (although you hint he was a liar), and his personal standards were such that on retirement, despite the offers from certain quarters of Fleet Street, he refused to say or write one word. Ask yourself how many senior detective police officers – or even parties in the Adams case – refused that kind of easy money or had those principles.

The stereotype of the CID officer giving evidence has always been of someone whose grammar and diction left something to be scoffed at and who fell into blushing and stammering confusion once faced with suave and wily counsel. I can well understand some counsel objected to his attitude, but why should a reporter find his desire to speak up so unwelcome?

When my father died, he left little money or other effects, and my mother, now seventy-nine, lives in the same rented flat they took over nearly fifty years ago. I wish now he had been opportunistic enough to make money when he had the chance. I find the final irony in that the money Adams bequeathed you was given to liver cancer research. It was cancer of the liver that took my much loved and admired father away from us.[94]

What lies beneath the words of this letter is a profile of a quiet, reserved, moderate man. Hannam did not court publicity and never really cared for celebrity. His grandson, Iain, in conversations with the present author, gave supporting information with regard to this. He recalls a man who was always self-contained and in control; he kept some cuttings and photos, but never initiated the kind of vanity enterprise, with an axe to grind, which has been the case with other participants in the major cases of Hannam's career. The man Iain Hannam describes was indeed ordinary and low-key in his private life; Iain recalls going to visit his grandfather on a Friday night, and watching his father and Bert play chess. The grandfather he knew was always smart, never dressed casually and always wore a tie; at that time, not long after retirement, Bert was living in Willesden, and just after retirement from the police he was in charge of security for the McAlpine firm. It is very much the mark and style of the man that, in his life in security work, he had a Rover 35 with a phone in it – a rare thing for the time. Bert, Iain recalls, had a sharp wit, liked to travel and was fundamentally a religious man; he relished being cross-examined, and loved to run rings around counsel in court.

He was surely proud of his son and grandson. In addition to being a commander, Kenneth was in charge of the training college where Bert had lectured later in his career. Iain said that Kenneth, too, fell foul of politics; he apparently made a speech at a Rotary club dinner in which he made some comments on the sometimes questionable relationship between politicians and the law, and allegedly there were 'backroom repercussions' to this. He was very likely blacklisted.

One ex-officer remembers meeting Kenneth in 1983, when he (the correspondent) was a clerical officer: 'He was often seen wandering the floors and often popped into our office for a chat or he would visit the map room to say hello. He was very friendly and I was very surprised when I found out he was a commander.' The same writer has a less than happy comment on Kenneth's farewell: 'Shortly after my arrival I and all the other staff were invited to his retirement party held at Tintagel House. It would have been in 1983/84; there were quite a few senior officers there of ACPO rank ... he gave a scathing speech, commenting how he had been treated in the last years of his service; he threw his warrant card which was picked up by one of the guests and passed around the room...' Another small insight into Kenneth has been given by Catherine Browne, who worked as a shorthand typist with Kenneth from 1967 onwards. She writes, 'He was tenacious and really had it in for the Victoria Sporting Club in Bayswater who he was convinced were using a roulette wheel with a double 36. After many raids a wheel was seized and taken ... it disappeared after a short time.' Iain Hannam also joined the police, attaining the rank of sergeant before he moved on to other things.

Speaking to Iain Hannam today, it is clear that Bert's career in the police must have influenced his son and grandson to follow suit. Similarly, while David Hewett did not follow in his father Charles' footsteps, he has remained knowledgeable and interested in police and legal matters. It is obvious that Hannam and Hewett left a legacy, and in a form far different from anything on paper or anything official. Their characters conveyed something fundamentally inviting and appealing about the profession.

Bert Hannam had learned his skills mostly on the job, but later, when the Training School was running efficiently, he was on the staff. Lesley Goddard, who graduated in 1981, wrote an account of the training in a special issue of a police publication: 'After you have finally completed Training School equipped with a warrant card, truncheon, whistle and notebook, and a vast amount of knowledge gleaned from the Instruction Book, you can at last start the job which you have been preparing for...'[95] She notes the wonderful feeling of becoming WPC Goddard rather than Cadet Goddard.

What was the role of the instructor, then? What exactly would Bert Hannam have done in that role? An interview with former detective Stuart Gibbon, who graduated at the same time as Lesley Goddard, provides some interesting insights. This account is from a time when Kenneth Hannam was a commander, and his portrait is included in the special edition brochure marking the graduation of cadets.

Hannam would have lectured. That was a basic duty of course. But this was the man who, in the course of the Adams trial, had said to the barrister Lawrence, 'If you will help me to help you sir...' Those are the words of a man who can meet fire with fire, and unsettle any opposition with apparent ease and savoir-faire. In a letter he wrote to Percy Hoskins, the man with considerable enmity towards him, we see this ability in action:

My Dear Percy,

Many thanks for your article in today's *Daily Express*. It is grand to find someone with two feet on the ground. The recent sensational publicity has caused me much anxiety and may incline to hamper our simple enquiry.

Thanks again,
Best wishes,
Bert Hannam[96]

The words 'simple enquiry' are a total contradiction of how Hoskins was to describe Hannam's work when he finally wrote about the case, decades afterwards. Bert Hannam was playing with the mind of his arch-enemy. We don't know at this point to what extent Hannam knew about Hoskins' sympathy with Adams, but he definitely knew about the common opinion of his reports on the investigations: concern at their bulk and thoroughness. He was fully aware that he could be criticized. We know full well how determined Hannam was to go ahead with the overall investigation, as this excerpt from the coroner's inquest on Bobbie Hullett shows:

> The coroner called again for Superintendent Hannam, who is a man of refined elegance and with silver grey hair.
>
> The Coroner: 'The Chief Constable of Eastbourne has called in Scotland Yard to enquire into the death of Mrs Hullett?'
>
> Hannam: 'Yes.'
>
> Coroner: 'Do you need any help with your work, or are there any reasons why you might call off your investigations?'
>
> Hannam: 'I appreciate your offer, but I have no wish to call off the investigations.'[97]

Conversations with people who knew him, including his grandson, have made it clear that this private man kept most of his memories to himself. But any account of Bert Hannam's life has to ask questions about the lacunae – the missing gaps. One nagging question concerns his acquisition of the specialist knowledge which was ascribed to him by the 1950s. The pastry cook was at first transmuted into the police officer; then the detective emerged, and in that capacity he became the Yard's top man when it came to a series of special, highly valued roles. These included, most significantly, his assistance to Wilfred Tarr in the late forties when his role in financial investigation was established. As the reporter in Halifax had noted, he had linguistic skills. It is clear that he learned from experience.

There are plenty of instances in which officers made rapid progress, being perceived to have rare qualities which were perfect for specific work. One of the clearest examples is that of Superintendent Albert Canning, who was assigned to head the spying on the movements of Wallis Simpson and her circle in 1935. He had been in the force only a very short time.

We have to conclude that Hannam was a man who had fundamental transferable skills, as we would call them today. He had an ability to learn quickly, to adapt to new challenges and situations, and to trust in hard work and application. After all, what most upset Percy Hoskins in the Adams case was, if we genuinely reflect on things written, that Hannam was indefatigable and determined to excel. It has already been noted that he could cope admirably with some of the finest legal brains in the land, so it has to be concluded that he learned efficiently and speedily, whether travelling in Europe with Inspector Tarr or applying himself to the minutiae of the financial legislation relevant to the currency regulation investigations.

He was also part of a fraternity. He was active in the years of hanging, when there was a retributive aspect to criminal investigation and legal process. Albert Pierrepoint explains this in his memoir of his work:

Not only the Manchester police were my pals. I had become very friendly with a number of the chiefs in Scotland Yard. I was having a drink one day in the Fitzroy tavern in Charlotte Street, Soho, which was kept by my friend Charlie Allchild, when he introduced me to a young CID officer in the Mets. This officer in turn

introduced me to Bob Fabian – 'Fabian of the Yard' – and we found
we got on very well.[98]

One thing we can know something about is what Hannam did as
a lecturer in the Police College. The enquiry into detective training
printed in the 1930s gives a full account of the curriculum as it existed
once Hendon was up and running from 1934, but matters were very
different twenty years later when he lectured, much as they had been
different in 1927 when he was a raw recruit. Back then Hannam had
been trained at Peel House, which held promotion exams for sergeants
and inspectors and in 1939 trained the 12,000 volunteer War Reserve
constables.[99] By the time of Hendon's heyday Peel House was used to
house officers. Brian Mills, recalling the sixties, notes that he knew
Peel House in its last year: 'The décor was pretty stark with tiled
walls, cream paint on the untiled parts and dark brown woodwork. It
was like going back to school.'

A retrospective feature in *The Times* in 1959 summarised the features
of the training as established in 1948 – the regime which Hannam
would have known and taught under. Hannam would have experienced
the Trenchard system, which was detailed and criticised by one writer:

Lord Trenchard often spoke in those days of 'mixing brains' as an
important part of his plans for the police college and he sought to
ensure this by having widely different types of student living and
working together. One of the original entrants, looking back across
25 years, describes that first entry as an extraordinary mixture. As
time went on ... it became more extraordinary; some considered
that the selectors laid too great an emphasis on skill in sport, others
that too little weeding out was done once men had got past the
selection board.[100]

In 1947, when his model for training was being replaced, Trenchard himself wrote to *The Times* to express his opinions:

> I think it is nothing less than disastrous to the police service to have dispensed with the fundamental basis of the Hendon Police College. I understand that on the expert committee set up under the chairmanship of Sir Frank Newsam there was not one single member who had passed through the Hendon Police College, or who had been an instructor at the college or even the Commandant. It must be remembered that some of the students of the College are now chief constables, and their views would have been valuable...[101]

When Hannam taught the recruits in the 1950s, it was immediately after the introduction of the new regime that Trenchard lamented as being far inferior to his own concept. This new approach placed the emphasis on lecturing and on solid study of the law books. Percy Hoskins, before he wrote his defence of Dr Bodkin Adams, produced a profusely illustrated guide to detective training as it was around 1950 when the new curriculum came in. There was an emphasis on dramatic roleplay, basic forensics and individual study. His guide, *No Hiding Place*, was 'the full authentic story of Scotland Yard in action' and was published by his own paper, the *Express*. Interestingly, the book includes pictures of various detectives, including William Chapman, Robert Lee, C. S. Hatherill and, of course, Robert Fabian, but no mention of Hannam or Hewett.

Detectives who have been through training school in more recent times stress that a great deal of time is spent in studying and practicing interview techniques, but in the 1930s, when a committee reported on detective training, there was practically no mention of the topic. This suggests that for Hannam, who was learning the skills of detective work just as the Trenchard approach was left behind, his learning 'on the job' would have put an emphasis on what would now be called the 'humanistic learning' inherent in a profession which involves dealing face to face with the public. It compares interestingly to a similar instance in legal training, in which a moot session introduces students to the interplay of personalities in an adversarial trial. The result of this is that when Hannam turned lecturer (and he was highly rated in this role) his knowledge had only ever been rooted in actual practice – hence the officer's letter to Hannam in chapter 2 in which he made reference to the importance of learning by actual experience.[102]

The regime at Hendon was basically an intensive sixteen-week course with military discipline. One graduate of 1981, Stuart Gibbon, recalled that the students referred to it as 'Colditz'. There was a perimeter security barrier and sergeants directed daily drilling; Gibbon admitted that the students felt fear and respect for the lecturers, and there was a definite distance between the two groups. The routine was hard work, in a room within one of three large residential blocks. Gibbon remembered his day being composed of intense book-learning, absorbing criminal law, along with study of the 'IB' – the Instruction Book. Much of the learning was 'word perfect' and the aim was to pass exams, with little time for socializing, although there were sports on offer. Wrapped around the study was the atmosphere of an army barracks, with boots being polished and uniforms ironed. Gibbon also brought up his sergeant, Brian Saunders, of whom he had a mix of fear and awe. There is no doubt that Bert Hannam would have been the type – much like Saunders – who injected humour into the lectures, but when it came to lunchtimes and breaks, the students would never approach the lecturers in any attempt to be friendly.

Trenchard was commissioner for just five years; he was an air marshal who had served in the Boer War and in Ireland. He had been commander of the Royal Flying Corps in the First World War and then played a major role in the creation of the RAF itself. His regime in the police brought about many radical changes, including bringing in a statistical department and a Daily Crime Telegram; he created a Detective Training School and a Police Scientific Laboratory. The training school at Hendon was his work, too. He was known to be reticent in discussing difficult matters like corruption in the force. He also challenged the policy, going back to the beginnings with Peel, of promoting from within. Trenchard saw the virtues of a short-service scheme. What Trenchard did was make the Police College the place where the real 'career men' would be trained and encouraged to use their talents, and to offer finite career periods to others. A short-term contract would allow a recruit to sign on for just ten years before retiring with a gratuity payment. His short-lived regime was assured some kind of continuity, however, as he appointed Sir Philip Game to succeed him – a man who could be relied on to act as if he were still an aide-de-camp.

In terms of purely detective work, the first training programme was begun in 1936 at Hendon. We have memoirs about how men became detectives, and these explanations help us to understand what the motivations were. A key element was discontentment with the beat work of the 'ordinary copper'. Leonard Nipper Read, for instance, 'the man who caught the Krays', explains it in that way, and says that the course at Hendon, which he attended in 1947, was 'drilling and lectures on public order, diseases of animals, child neglect, company fraud, incest, rape, bigamy, sodomy, helping children at school crossings, suicide, infanticide, drunks, ponces and traffic control'. Read started as a detective when a senior officer said he had a job for him and that he would be working in plain clothes.

Before the new training, though, a bright policeman – or a restless one – followed a set procedure of application to become a detective. This is explained in a biography of Detective Inspector Nixon:

> He outlined the routine. An applicant wrote his name in the book provided for the purpose in the Station. In due course, as vacancies occurred, if he were considered by the Station Detective Sergeant as a possibility his name was forwarded through the usual channels and he was interviewed by the Divisional Detective Inspector. If the interview was satisfactory the applicant was posted for CID duties as an 'aide' when he was tried out on his own...[103]

Read was a man who went through that process twenty years later, and he explains that as an aide the idea was that you had a mentor. He began at St John's Wood and there his mentor was Martin Walsh, of whom Read wrote: 'I was put under the wing of one of the best detectives I have ever met ... He was an older man, in his forties, who was used as a "tutor" aide. He taught me what investigating was all about.' In that way, Nixon and Read learned to be detectives by working on the streets with experienced men. But what about the new men going to the college?

A great deal can be learned about that curriculum from the 1938 *Report of the Departmental Committee on Detective Work and Procedure*. That report outlines the whole course of training, from a review of general detective work, through to specific skills such as crime record-keeping and photography. The document was produced by a team led by Sir Samuel Hoare, Secretary of State for the Home Office. In terms of commentary on existing detective work, the report puts considerable emphasis on communication between individual officers and indeed at the group operational level, as in comments about detectives from different forces gathering to exchange information at race meetings. Men asked in the course of the enquiry had repeatedly suggested that detective work would be notably improved if a 'spirit of co-operation was fostered'.

The 1930s was the time at which it was properly acknowledged that communication across the country among the authorities was crucially important in police work, and the report recommends bringing senior officers from different forces together so that they can work together at the earliest opportunity in the process of investigating a specific crime. The normal practice at the time, if a man had to go to work in another area, was for the officer to notify the CID concerned, but the report's authors noted a very uneven application of this principle. They advised individual procedures but stressed that an effective system of intelligence about criminals was at the top of the list of requirements. In the years immediately before the 1938 report, 'lending' of officers had been very small scale, and it is clear that these instances were for particular expertise; just twenty lendings took place in the years between 1931 and 1936. Naturally, in murder cases, this kind of lending activity is more important, and the authors report that the recent results were encouraging:

In the five years 1931–35 there were known to the police 460 cases of murder or suspected murder of persons aged one year or over (others were infanticide since 1922). In 181 of these cases the murderer ... committed suicide, leaving 279 cases to be detected ... arrests were made in 254 cases...[104]

Training of officers received close attention. After all, numbers of officers were accelerating quickly and the force was huge compared to the Ripper years, just five decades before. In 1938 there were 1,198 CID personnel; Liverpool and Birmingham had equivalent forces of over a hundred men. As recruitment was clearly increasing, it was a good time to take stock of needs and of methods. All the obvious issues were discussed in the course of exploring the nature of the detective needed in that time of inter-war expansion of organised crime, rackets and robberies. One of the central points considered was the idea of a probationary period, a similar idea to the 'aide' system. The panel concluded that no probation was needed but conceded that a detective is 'always on probation' in that he or she must always be 'subject to continuing to discharge duties successfully'.

The syllabus for training recommended in the report was based on the question of integration or separation from the normal police training syllabus. The decision was that a thirteen-week course was necessary for detective recruits. In addition to that, the decision was for recruits to spend six weeks attached to a CID as in the aide system. In terms of the content of the syllabus, this is, in summary form, the course decided on:

Week 1: Conduct and professionalism; dealing with the press; prevention of crime; co-operative detective work; use of scientific aids; intelligence reports; local knowledge; observation and special contexts for work.

Week 2: Fingerprints; judges' rules; telephone and wireless; use of cars; photography; searching scene of crime.

Week 3: Legal knowledge – summonses; warrants; powers of arrest; identification parades; prisoners' rights; larceny; receivers; housebreaking notation and study of scene; robbery.

Week 4: Sexual offences; knowledge of obscene publications; infanticide.

Week 5: Homicide law; scene-of-crime photography; coroners and inquests; wounds; blood groups; poisoning; explosives offences; arson; financial fraud and fraud in use of materials.

Week 6: Bribery and corruption; blackmail; Official Secrets Acts; procedure in courts; reports to other forces.

Week 7: Dangerous drugs; courts; extradition.

Week 8: Depositions; dying declarations; testimony of the sick.

This is, as would be expected, very thorough and wide-ranging. Police work expands and becomes more complex as a population increases and the knock-on effects of industrial and urban growth continue. At the time of that report, all manner of recent developments were absorbed into the thinking behind that syllabus. To take one example, the first Official Secrets Act was passed in 1911, but there had been a second one in 1920 and a third was in preparation as this report was written, becoming statute law the next year, in 1939. A detective would have to become acquainted with such topics as knowing which places were prohibited and why, and to whom; how communication of classified information could or would be passed; and how to access accommodation addresses of suspects. Another example of the complexity and also the delicacy of the knowledge absorbed is the awareness of the 'dying declaration'. It was not uncommon, in the age well before motorways, for a police officer to find him or herself in an ambulance on the way to hospital with a dying victim of a murderous attack. The dying declaration would be crucially important and would need to be written verbatim. In one case, an old man had been beaten almost to death by two assailants in a lonely farmhouse; he talked in the ambulance to the police officer about the attackers' accents, saying they sounded Chinese. That detail would prove crucial in the ensuing investigation.

One very important topic approached by the report was the ongoing issue of records. There were, of course, ever-growing records in all counties and areas, and the authors of the committee report saw the central importance of this being rationalised and also unified in terms of method and control. It might have been stating the obvious, but the point was made that 'it is important that the functions of the Criminal Record Office should not be assumed by any regional record centre' and that a Main Fingerprint Index should be maintained. The Clearing House system would be maintained and reviewed, in order to make sure that the right information was directed to the right places.

What about the more people-centred aspects of the new detective work? One of the most enlightening examples of this is in the details about photography in the report. An appendix goes into specific detail about what procedure must be observed by the detective using photography for records. There are technical drawings of all equipment and very particular images of the chair on its turntable. The basis of this work is the maintenance of the card index record. This had ten sections of information to be listed in the right places. After that, there are seven categories of index described. If we add to this the expected knowledge of publications and the updating of basic criminological knowledge, then the work of the detective could easily become 'paperwork', so we have to ask about the supposed excitement and appeal of the profession at that time. The answers are in a study by Percy Hoskins, referred to previously. In his richly illustrated guide to detective training as it was around 1955, Hoskins gives a clear idea of how that conception in the report of twenty years earlier had become a workable system. *No Hiding Place* is a feel-good advert for Scotland Yard, but it explains all the intricacies of the work for the layperson.

Hoskins' hypothetical detective recruit begins with his thirteen weeks at Peel House. He then becomes a detective recruit for a year, before moving on to Hendon. The basis is practical all the way: 'The paramount need for keen observation is again drilled into the men's heads. The theory of the Yard is that a good description is better than any picture and its detectives are taught to cultivate retentive memories as a matter of routine.' Then the recruit is faced with the more academic side of work – criminal law, for instance. The practice then was for both senior detectives and lawyers working in prosecution.

Hoskins interviewed Commander Rawlings, deputy of the CID, about detective work and the reply was, 'It is 95 per cent perspiration, 3 per cent inspiration and 2 per cent luck!' On top of all the good advice and legal material, Hendon was equipped with all kinds of devices for simulation of events, and every aid for information processing. These were materials relating to subject maps, facial characteristics, observation tests, scale models, anatomy, basic ballistics and forgery methods. The simulation training entailed hypothetical cases, and these were often printed in the *Police Review*, which had been published since 1893, the intention being that all officers could and should constantly update their skills and keep sharp. A typical simulation would be in these stages:

1. The discovery of a body. A tyre-mark is close to it.

2. Recruit uses two-way radio for assistance and takes measurements

3. The body is then examined for hair, stains etc.

4. Photography is then used for things such as tyre marks.

5. Witnesses are interviewed

6. Enquiries made in adjacent buildings

7. Clues are then taken to the laboratory

8. As the forensics take place, the trainee traces owner of the car

9. The owner is selected at an identity parade.

It all seems very simple, but in essence that sequence of events inevitably draws in a number of specialists; it entails skills of verbal communication, and it calls for a sense of close observation and deduction from available knowledge.

As for the more modern concepts and elements of detective work, some of the principal ones were around in the 1950s but not in operation or even generally accepted. For instance, offender profiling was conceived by Dr James Brussel in 1956 after a bomb explosion in a cinema in Brooklyn. It was the work of a criminal dubbed 'the Mad Bomber'. Brussel had worked with the CIA and the FBI on profiling in the war, and on studying the case notes he went to work on profiling the Mad Bomber. The doctor listed ten important features of the criminal, including the note that the man had 'an Oedipus complex'. Sure enough, a man was tracked down after a phone call.

But for more practical, people-centred detective skills, one of the most criticised elements of training then was interviewing technique. This situation had been exacerbated by prominent murder cases in which suspects who have emerged as mentally ill or with learning difficulties have produced 'confessions' after interviewing. One remarkable case was in 1946, when two Scotland Yard detectives came north to the Lincolnshire area and interviewed a man on suspicion of murder. His housekeeper had been battered to death and investigation had opened up no other potential suspects. He had a mental age of fifteen, yet a linguistically somewhat advanced confession was produced. But for the work of a talented and strong-willed barrister, the man would quite probably have hanged.

Training began in some old huts in Hendon, and remained there except for a spell at Peel House. Obviously, training today has a high level of technology involved; but a report published in *Police Review* in June 2006 indicates that the CID is no longer seen as a glamorous job and new strategies are being used to attract recruits. Certainly, back in 1936 there was an element of glamour; but Hoskins' work relies heavily on the appeal of some of the features that had made life in the services appealing to many in the war: advanced communications, fast cars, efficient firepower, physical confrontation – and, of course, a sense of a moral crusade against the 'forces of evil and anarchy' as implied in the magazines and comics.

The detective had been a figure in print and in illustration since the 1920s, inspired by real operators such as Allan Pinkerton. In addition, America's organised crime explosion during Prohibition years, and the 'private dick' of the black-and-white crime films, and in the new talkies, had an impact in Britain. The fictional men Sam Spade and Philip Marlowe were there in celluloid and in print, private detectives, but there were also the Yard men, and the Flying Squad had made a detective career not only glamorous but dramatic – just the thing in 1945 to attract the types who had lived through thrilling times and travelled across the world only to come home to the nine-to-five. At the time of the report into detective training, crimes novels set in England were selling prolifically: Ngaio Marsh's Inspector Alleyn first appeared in *A Man Lay Dead* in 1934; Agatha Christie created Superintendent Battle in *The Secret of Chimneys* (1925); and Leo Bruce's Sergeant Beef appeared in *A Case for Three Detectives* in 1936.

Developing the role of detective in the years 1930 to 1960 meant a constant series of revisions in working methods and also in personnel – the types of men who came along at the right time to use their talents well. The next logical step was to take the CID out of 'the Smoke' and into the regions, and that is where we will meet Leonard Nipper Read again. The strictures in the 1930s as regards communication with the regional forces gradually attained more importance. The old cry of 'Send for Scotland Yard' became more and more common as crimes grew more violent and ruthless in the burgeoning new towns and the troubled Victorian ones. That call had been going on in a sense even before there was a Scotland Yard – since 1834, when people from a village in Wiltshire asked for help from 'Bow Street'. A pattern was established, and it is almost mythic. First there is a murder or a high-level robbery; then the local police do all the conventional things but remain stumped. Clearly, the more sophisticated officers in London will help, so call them in. Even the amateurs in fiction were called out for local horrors, the archetype being, arguably, Sherlock Holmes going out to Dartmoor to sort out the ravages caused by the Hound of the Baskervilles.

Inspector Nixon, quoted above, makes a useful comparison with Bert Hannam. Starting in 1921 but recruited eventually into the Thames River Police, the course of his career reflected Hannam's in many ways. He offers his readers so much about his learning curve and his peers that today his writing is invaluable in helping us put together the kind of training Hannam would have experienced.

The regime would have suited Hannam very well; he was a man who, although he had a keen sense of humour, was fully aware of the need to be aloof and maintain a respectful distance in the learning process. After all, the course was a mix of classroom work and roleplay, and in the latter, which entailed work being done in a mock-police station with constructed 'incidents' to practice on, every test entailed the student being observed and marked by a man with a clipboard close by.

In his long police career, Hannam had tasted experience in a number of divisions and special operations, including E, X, Y and D areas. He was a Londoner through and through, and there would have been very little terrain around the city that he did not know well. By the time he was drafted in to lecture and guide the tyros in the force, he had wide experience not only of the topography of his home city, but also of the diverse subcultures and the oppositions, attitudes and prejudices of such a mixed population.

The contrast cannot be more marked between Hannam the ace detective with a highly unusual casebook and his 'afterlife', in which his reputation was only scantily assessed. For instance, in memoirs he has been repeatedly criticised, and often for his virtues. Keith Simpson, who knew him at the same time as Molly Lefebure, during and just after the war, wrote of him that 'the Sussex police ... called for help from Scotland Yard ... Detective Superintendent Herbert Hannam, a very unusual sort of policeman, was sent to make enquiries. Well dressed, possibly slightly conceited, confident, certainly well aware of his powers and not without experience (though hardly of this kind of scandal) Hannam set out to get to the bottom of the affair.'[105] Reading between the lines here, are we to conclude that our law officers should lack confidence and be simply 'normal' – whatever the adjective 'unusual' means here?

Even worse for its descriptions of Hannam in action is Frankie Fraser's memoir, in which he does nothing but reiterate the distortions of the true crime magazines, summing up the Bodkin Adams fiasco on the chance meeting, in this way, 'What's come out over the years is that it wasn't just verballing, but they had a thing called scriptwriting. If there was a bank-job or a hi-jack, something like that, then there'd be one officer whose job it was to write up a script giving all the coppers their parts to play...'[106]

Now, this is no more than a repeat of an urban myth, all material handed down unthinkingly from an oral tradition. Yet it stands in print, giving a cynical view, entirely opposite to DS Hewett's explanation. As in the opening of this chapter, the image of the doll's house still persists: in the rooms of Hannam's life, there is little available to confirm for us which ones he preferred, but his habitation in that house was always somehow easy and comfortable. He was imperturbable and, as far as may be ascertained, very difficult to shift from attitudes and opinions. He made an exceptional detective because he knew where to look and what questions to ask, and of whom. He also had the virtue of remaining silent, allowing the silences to speak for themselves. One suspects that an opinion was a dangerous, questionable thing by his habits of thought. A fact was far more desirable.

There is also what we read between the lines in his few words given during investigations. The Emily Pye case, for instance, gives us some clues; there were 97,000 local people who were aware of his actions and appeals, but only a handful of responses emerged. His few words among the energetic enquiries show just how profoundly he wanted to find the despicable individual who had mercilessly killed a tiny old lady for the profit of a few pounds. The local photos for the Yorkshire press show him in certain rather dramatic poses, and this, combined with his smart attire, belie his genuine access to the local problems and difficulties he encountered. Once again, persistence and thoroughness were his watchwords.

The press always wanted him to be the 'character', the one who stood out as eccentric and 'colourful', and one suspects that he cultivated that image. An interesting context for this can be found in an aspect of the twentieth century up until the 1970s: the universality of occupational and leisure uniforms. Distinctive dress was inherited from the Victorian and Edwardian ages, and it is obvious when one watches old black-and-white documentaries that virtually every walk of life entailed distinctive dress. Being smart and presentable was obligatory: it informed the public that the person had a role and a responsibility. Hannam's smartness and the dashing appearance were his own version of this, and contrasted powerfully with the image of detectives in popular culture, for instance the bedraggled untidiness of Philip Marlowe.

How are we to assess this quiet man, then? What is there between the lines in print that might lead us to evaluate his life as a detective fairly and objectively? The opinions and brief profiles of him in print are either misleading or simply regurgitate the usual rather thoughtless views given elsewhere. One answer is that the man himself is truly visible through his friendships – his sergeants as well as his superiors, and his peers in the training school as much as those he worked with and mixed with socially. But it is also in the people who placed a distance between themselves and Hannam that we see important aspects of him too. Percy Hoskins includes in his book *No Hiding Place* the chest-beating proclamation that 'Percy Hoskins has been described as Scotland Yard's "Dr Watson". In twenty-six years as a crack Fleet Street crime reporter for the London *Daily Express*, Hoskins has watched the tracking down of most of the notorious murderers of our time.'[107] In no circumstances did Hannam produce such an item of vanity. In modern parlance, Hoskins was 'branding' himself for the media. He was also taking sides. Hence in his book on current crime and detectives there was no place for Bert Hannam, who never courted familiarity and fellowship in Fleet Street. If he did, there is no Hoskins to act as his Boswell.

In the end Hannam has to be assessed through his achievements, and these are impressive; he will probably always be looked at through the prism of the Bodkin Adams case, but that more than distorts, and it also provides merely a voice and a few dialogues. Paradoxically, Hannam's actions communicate far more in some ways, such as his reliance on community enquiries. As Pamela Cullen put it, 'Hannam inaugurated a new procedure for questioning every householder in the area. Each detective had a printed questionnaire to be filled in by the detective himself, with seventeen questions... Hannam had to be patient and not overlook anything.'[108] It was this utter thoroughness which marked him out. He would have been very successful in commercial marketing or in espionage.

Finally, we now have, thanks to the material being printed in Pamela Cullen's book, the contents of Hannam's letters written to his colleagues, and from these much may be gleaned on his character. They were mostly written to C. S. Findlay, and they reveal a man who was extremely sensitive to the press in his work. In one note, he reports on the question of exhumation at a time when there was feverish activity about the possibility of various former patients of Dr Adams being exhumed in a search for evidence regarding poison: 'This afternoon several of the press fellows have worried me about their own references to exhumations ... I saw four of them and said, "The question of any exhumation has not arisen, it may never arise and no thought can be given to such a possibility until the enquiries are more advanced and their results studied."'[109] He also made it clear that he wanted to keep his distance from them. Hannam was acutely aware of the callous intrusions of reporters, such as their offers of money to cemetery staff for information. We know now that the famous pathologist Dr Francis Camps had gone to talk with Hannam in Eastbourne about the subject of exhumation, and in this context it is also plain that the press had fabricated matters supposedly relating to his work, such as the statement that 'soil samples taken from the Ocklinge cemetery, where Mrs Bradnum is buried, have been examined by Dr Camps'. Hannam wrote in his notes that this was 'quite untrue'.[110]

The Bert Hannam revealed in these letters is every inch the dutiful, sensitive investigator, aware of the potential harm that could be done by media intrusion to any ongoing police search for solid evidence.

10

A SUMMING-UP

All biographical sources – mostly in oral history and memoir – state that Hannam was a reserved, quiet man, and this is at odds with the way in which he has been portrayed by the press throughout the 1950s when he was something of a celebrity. The reporters enjoyed his oddness, his eccentricity, as they saw it. In fact, these are the wrong words to apply to him. He was an assertive individual, colourful in dress and personality, in a drab time.

Bert Hannam was never entirely and savagely attacked, but he was criticized, and he took it on the chin. This may be seen several years after his prominence in the Adams and Whiteway cases, in a paragraph in *The Spectator*, in which we have this:

I see that Superintendent Hannam of Bodkin Adams fame (if fame is the word) has been giving his recipe for a good policeman. His first ingredient is courage, which seems unexceptionable; but the precise type of courage which Superintendent Hannam finds so essential seems a little odd. It is 'the courage to do things the law forbids'. I must say that after the Towpath case and the Adams case I had my doubts as to how far Superintendent Hannam was a really good policeman. But I am sure he has always been courageous – and for that matter consistent.

There is something wryly offensive about this, as if the anonymous writer wants to dig up the contentious past simply to keep a slur on a man's reputation. But Hannam lived with these attitudes, and one suspects he thrived on them.

As noted earlier, he emerged as a detective at a time when there were widespread public concerns about crime. In late 1945, *The Times* ran a feature with the heading 'Defeating the Criminal' and reported on a talk by Sir Harold Scott, Commissioner of Police, who had called a press conference at the Yard to discuss a 'crime wave' in the land. Scott's attitude was summarised thus: 'In this regard he mentioned the recent so-called crime wave. While he would be the last to say it was not serious, there were many people who had now got the impression that London was now like some lawless place in the Middle West of America years ago.' He gave the press some alarming figures: in London in 1945 there had been 471 burglaries, 6,192 house-breakings, 11,950 shop break-ins, 299 robberies and assaults, 32,000 simple larcenies, and, last but not least, 32 murders. His heartening news was that 'detectives are working very long hours and doing an extraordinarily good job'.

This was Hannam's world of work as he reached twenty years of service. The landscape was grim after the depredations of the war, as is vividly described in a memoir by Ian Thomson:

That part of London was a frightful 'midden' [dunghill] and so run down ... The square below her window was full of smoke-dunned Georgian terraces, once smart but now the borderlands of the East End. Canonbury had been knocked about in the war. In many places the pavements and terrace walls were still cracked from doodlebugs. Some walls were held up by large wooden beams, windows remained smashed ...

Yet there are wider issues relating to detective work. Detectives are perceived as leading the counter-attack against the threat of disorder and anarchy. The theory goes that in narratives of crime, the reader wants to believe in the bourgeois illusion of rationality – in other words, that the good guy wins and the bad guy is punished. Who is in the vanguard of the defence of this rationality? The detective. Such is the prevalence of this notion that such thinking goes well beyond Sherlock Holmes and Inspector Morse. Tag the word 'detective' on someone and the moral implications follow, along with the expected qualities of physical courage, lack of fear and, perhaps most of all, a special knowledge of the enemy – of how disorder and anarchy thrive, together with knowledge of how they can be stopped.

There are some unanswered questions and some gaps in my narrative: the shift from pastry cook to police officer is the first one. After that, the biography has presented problems familiar to any writer assembling the data of a life. These include dealing with the usual tantalising snippets or references to offshoots from the main thread of the life under scrutiny. Not the smallest of these has been the European work Hannam undertook, which for now has to lie in the dark, overshadowed by the homicide cases.

In reading the foregoing pages, the question surely occurs to the reader: why are police officers' memoirs so rare, so limited in scope? One answer is that it is a profession strangely contained in the minimal and fleeting record of the notebook. Other than that, the casebook each officer has known is stored inside the computer system. Case follows rapidly on case. Traditionally, top-brass detectives at the Yard have given very predictable reasons for recording their experience. However, some have written the memoir and given no reason at all, as was the case with Hugh Young, Commander at the CID, whose book *My Forty Years at the Yard* contains no explanation of why he wrote. The usual pattern in such publishing is that a specific detective gains a certain notoriety when linked to a sensational crime, and there is pressure on him to write a memoir. Of course, what happens is that accounts of the more mundane duties of detection and the process of police work are eclipsed by the sensational, and the more overtly documentary elements are given short shrift by the media.

My summing-up should offer a satisfactory conclusion, as readers will now know much more about a rather enigmatic sleuth, but once can also sense a teasing shadow cast over the pages by Bert Hannam – a tormenting shadow, reminding everyone that something in him was completely satisfied with the record of his life in the newspapers and magazines. In so many interviews with people in my writing life, I have met the attitude of '*Who would be interested in my life?*' It would be so easy to imagine the Count saying that, as he moves his chess piece to win the game.

I have been constantly mindful of the fact that a biography can only offer an interpretation, and that is from selected or available facts; the more direct and candid narrative may be hidden from view and will always remain so. But in Hannam's case the evidence when we investigate him, the man who was always the investigator, is solid and does not fall open to speculation or to revisions.

Some biographies fall into the category of thematic, and the chronology is less important, but it has become clear that Hannam's life is best rendered in the phases of learning and experience that he absorbed. At the heart of it all there are the courtroom confrontations.

Writers on criminology have had much to say on the strategies of lawyers in court, and in our age of ubiquitous theoretical reference to every aspect of the criminal law and its application, we have statement such as this: 'Barristers ... have stock storytelling strategies available to them, the power of which is sometimes enhanced by the judge advising the jury to use their common sense in deciding on their verdict.'[111] Hannam was caught up in such adversarial trials, and the interesting aspect of this is that he had no direct training on that aspect of his job, other than advice from senior officers – if there was any given, of course.

For reasons such as this, the Hannam the reader has met here became the kind of detective he wanted to be largely by fashioning his own persona from the precepts and habits he gained early on. My own view is that his work on currency regulation was a profound influence on this, because he was taken out of his comfort zone, as it were, to learn 'on his feet' and cope. After being prominent in such a trial, a murder case would not have been such a challenge. The work he did for the Treasury had to entail the kind of activity that earns the abuse and disgust of the public.

In Hannam's last few years as a policeman, in the late 1950s, one could easily point to significant social problems which led to extreme criminal activity. Yes, societal issues contributing to crime could arguably be identified for any age, such as the epidemic of garrotter-gang crime in the 1860s, but at Hannam's point of departure for a different life, away from villains and manhunts, British society had a crisis in certain categories of crime and of police engagement with new versions of old offences. As Hannam was busy with Alfred Whiteway and the Towpath murders, for instance, a twenty-year-old named Michael Davies was convicted as the perpetrator of the Clapham Common Murder. It was a gangland crime, and the result was a death sentence. Davies was due to die on 11 November, but then there was a postponement and an appeal. This failed to save his neck, and so a new date was fixed for the hanging. After that, in part due to a huge petition for his reprieve, he was spared and given a life sentence.

This was the Teddy Boy era, with its large-scale gang conflicts, and these disturbances intermingled with race riots. As far as the police were concerned everything was in hand to deal with the 'Teds', but we may glean the scale of the problem when we look at one case, summarised by Michael Macilwee, who has made a special study of this phenomenon: 'More than 5,000 Chingford residents had signed a petition calling for the Home Secretary to deal with the Teddy Boys – they were, they said, concerned for the safety of their children after dark.'[112] The top Yard men met and conferred, and then put into practice the measures of the 1936 Public Order Act and began a ruthlessly tough war on the gangs. Authority was being challenged, and openly. My own life stretches back to schooldays in the 1950s, and when I was eleven, in 1959, a gang of twenty 'Teds' arrived at the gates of my secondary modern school to challenge our teachers to a fight. They got one. Staff poured out of the staffroom and won the scrap, fighting against knives and chains.

Hannam retired as these new crises were boiling over; although there would always be murder cases and tabloid campaigns pinpointing alleged police failings, he would have known that the Yard detective would always be there, as a figurehead and a sign of reassurance that all would be well now that the professionals were on the scene. It had been that way in Britain since the days before any permanent, regulated police force, and the only real difference between the situation around 1800 and in 1960 was that by the latter date the suspicions of a 'police state' were gone.

Bert Hannam had served thirty-three years. In that time there had, of course, been a world war, and then a period of privation in which the resilience of the nation was severely tested. There was also great social unrest throughout that time, with the 1929 economic crisis biting hard. Hannam was a young officer when the Jarrow Crusade men walked into London, and when the Black Shirts stirred up violence in the streets. As he left, the cultural revolution that would shake up every level of society was just beginning. After those demanding decades, in which he had faced the forces of disorder and dissolution, he was entitled to supervise the security of McAlpine's building sites and advise on better protection and preservation of resources. That was, and still is, a viable option for a police officer on retirement; it may have been bland after such adventures in criminal investigation as he had known, but it was a job. He was too young for the pipe and slippers.

Whenever Hannam's name was mentioned, someone in the media world took up the offer of a commentary on him. His presence in sensational cases drew him into tabloid notoriety, and references to him veered between 'Hannam of the Yard' and 'the Count', with the added rather obvious moniker of 'Hannam of Bodkin Adams fame'. For his part he gave them few rods, keeping his statements mostly factual and analytical, giving little away.

Fred Cherrill, a fingerprint expert at the Yard and a contemporary of Hannam, wrote of the force he loved so much that 'one of the greatest obstacles to getting a 100-per-cent efficient police force is the difficulty of maintaining the interest and keenness of officers until the end of their service, whatever rank they may have attained. I feel that the man on the beat is in need of a continued incentive if he is not to develop into an automaton.'[113] As a final comment on Bert Hannam, it has to be asserted that neither his incentive to improve nor his motivation ever flagged.

Appendix 1

'EASING THE PASSING':
HISTORICAL PERSPECTIVES

The Bodkin Adams case throws up some interesting topics which, though not germane to any argument in my text, need some attention and comment. Such is the depth of the layers of reference and implication for the state of medicine at the time that some further cognisance needs to be given to the academic writing which relates to the Adams case. It is helpful to first move a long way back through the years to a significant cultural trend which is discernible over a century before Dr Adams.

In 1834, in a religious publication for children, we have the following:

I was with her a few hours before she died. Her sufferings at that time seemed to be severe. About twenty minutes before she expired, she appeared to be easy, and enquired for her father, her master, and a few friends, and took her final leave of them in a very affecting manner. She then died in the Lord, with as much tranquillity as if she had fallen into a natural sleep...[114]

This may be a suitable account of the dying process if a certain level of propaganda and reassurance is required, but in reality death and dying present little more than a period of extreme physical pain and fear of a nature previously unknown to the sufferer.

The Christian 'good death' may have been a standard trope of Victorian and Edwardian times, but in reality the medical rather than the spiritual presence at the deathbed is extremely prominent, and by the 1950s dying at home in one's bed was something which, as memories and anecdote show, played no part in any approach to death within the new National Health Service, which entailed a perfunctory, supervised exit in a hospital ward.

Alongside the National Health Service structures and methodology, there was the persistence of the local family GP. This figure is familiar in modern literature in the stories of A. J. Cronin and Richard Gordon. In characters like Dr Cameron and Dr Finlay, on radio and on television, the image of the family doctor who shows concern by going to excessive lengths to look after their patients is deeply embedded in the national psyche, and it can be seen at work in the manner in which the press took up the case of Dr Adams. Pictures in the popular press showed him on visits, walking in Eastbourne; but that could easily be transmuted into a gothic image of 'Dr Death' as the gossip and tittle-tattle increased – hence the uneasy relationship between the caring doctor archetype and the doctor who helped one to shuffle off this mortal coil in a heroin-induced coma.

The Victorian attitudes, based on the certainty of heaven and forgiveness in most cases, meant that in popular culture images of the deathbed were rife with symbolism, read in the language of flowers and other paraphernalia. By the inter-war years, this had become a hot topic. One may argue that the decline of religious belief after the First World War is a factor. There had been widespread death, both in the war itself and also in the massive Spanish flu epidemic of 1918. The visibility of this mass death did not marry well with former conceptions of young death. The notion of sacrifice percolated into the ideology of young servicemen, but back home it seemed to many that God had deserted His people. One oral history project done in the 1970s records a Bradford woman commenting, 'So many young men were taken away in our street that my mother stopped believing in a good Lord. She never went to church again.'[115]

When it comes to medical professionals and their relationships and interactions in wards and homes, some contemporary documentary sources help us to grasp the kinds of attitudes that existed between staff as regards the care of the dying in the 1950s. For instance, this is an extract from a nurse's notebook from the 1940s:

Honour all staff nurses and G.P.'s that thy days may be long in the uniform the association provided for thee. In fear the clever medico should ask her things she does not know ... Now, who is this at last we see – the faulty past – but memory is really fully blown...[116]

This is from the notebook of a nurse who worked in private homes with doctors. Part of a list of tongue-in-cheek observations about her working life, it touches on the underlying attitude during the proceedings in the Adams case when those nurses were examined by Lawrence and clearly hints at the power relationships existing then.

In fact, the Adams case highlights a very important subject in medico-legal history: terminal care in post-war Britain. Caitlin Mahar's prize-winning essay 'Easing the Passing' won the Roy Porter Student Essay Prize in 2012 for its examination of this subject. Mahar looks at the wider implications of the Adams case and the doctor's attitudes to what we now call palliative care. The principal subject is what was seen as the necessity of 'easing the passing' as a humanitarian measure when pain was not to be erased or suppressed with anything in the armoury of the general practitioner except morphine. The experts in court in the Adams case found difficulty in matching what was common practice with their own rules about acceptable use. Hence the shock for Dr Douthwaite when he learned of what had been done in Cheshire in the treatment of Mrs Morrell.

Mahar's essay throws light on the nature of treatment and drug use in cases of terminal illness both at the time of the Adams case and earlier. The conclusions confirm the general suspicion that taking a life was unofficially sanctioned, in spite of the Hippocratic oath – and, of course, in spite of the law. The easing of insufferable pain took priority over the aim to preserve life in all circumstances.[117] The classic wording of the oath in this respect is: 'I will neither give a deadly drug to anybody who asks for it, nor will I make a suggestion to this effect.' There is nothing ambiguous about that.

Mahar looked into previous work in this area and the results were most relevant to Bodkin Adams' practice and his habits over many years. The summary of the situation regarding the drugs given by Adams is contextualised by Mahar very helpfully: 'Caution was paramount. Concerned that pain relief that precipitated death was illegal, violated the medical duty to preserve life and risked eroding the trust of patients and families, nineteenth-century physicians warned against the administration of such drugs.' This is then contrasted with the 1950s situation: 'Between the 1930s and the 1950s, "Brompton mixtures", which were to become a central component in the work of the modern hospice movement, were widely prescribed to those deemed terminal in religious and charitable homes as well as hospitals.'[118]

Clearly, the important point here, which underlies much of the cut and thrust of the action in the Adams trial, is that an individual decided on what was 'deemed terminal'. In the Adams case, that individual was

Dr Bodkin Adams. Here was a man who, compared with his relatives in the medical field – notably his brilliant uncle Dr John Bodkin, who was a very bright medico and went to work as a missionary in China – had not exactly shone as a star graduate. Yes, he had worked hard to gain his diplomas in public health and in anaesthetics, but the impression we have is that he was more a steady workhorse than a prize stallion in his profession. Some felt at the time that the power to decide when someone could be helped along to eternity would give such a man a grandiose sense of his own importance. On such a line of thought did much of the activity of the press depend, and it would have been on the minds of many at the trial.

Clifford Hoyle, writing in a medical journal in 1944, produced the memorable phrase, 'The law forbids in theory but ignores in practice.'[119] One interesting clinical note regarding what was actually administered comes from a dictionary of 1934, which Adams would certainly have known and used: 'For delirium and the sleeplessness of fever, hyoscine, chloral hydrate, and chloralamide are generally employed, and for sleeplessness with no assignable cause, veronal, trional or sulphanol is perhaps best, and is not attended by the risk of starting a habit which is hard to break.'[120] But of course much depends on the prognosis behind the treatment; if the end of life is considered to be imminent, then a clear case for euthanasia is present. From the above it is clear that Hannam's persistent and determined gathering of facts and potential evidence rocked a very large boat.

In the end, comparisons with Harold Shipman might offer something useful. One assessment, by Martin Fido, is indicative of one influential opinion:

It would be expected that his routine taking of human life was a manifestation of power, of his will to play God and exercise ultimate control over who should be given life and who should be given death. That, of course, is what he did, but that was not his motive. He was too ordinary, too bland, too boring to assign himself such a grand role.[121]

That was said of Shipman, and one has to compare what we know of Adams to that last sentence. He was arguably the exact opposite, cultivating quite a stylish, culturally impressive figure in the upper circles of Eastbourne society.

Very much in the minds of the British Medical Council was the announcement made in October 1950 that doctors had barred mercy killing. The World Medical Association had said this, and Dr Gregg, a British doctor, said openly that 'many doctors had used drugs to speed the death of incurable patients suffering great pain'. The world's doctors had declared that it was in the public interest, as well as being in line with natural and civil rights, that euthanasia be banned.[122]

Everyone around the Adams trial, at the higher levels of the judiciary and the police, was surely fully aware of the recent debates in the upper echelons of the medical establishment; the whole topic cast a shadow over the events of the trial, and the papers kept reporting matters in a tone as sensational as that for the reportage on the euthanasia furore at its most emotional in the mid- to late 1930s.

Appendix 2

CHARLES HEWETT BY DAVID HEWETT

During my research for this book, David Hewett, Charles' son, was kind enough to offer some reflections on the Hannam–Hewett friendship and professional partnership. This was all of substantial help to me, as DS Hewett had been an important participant in the Bodkin Adams investigation and, in my opinion, has never received due consideration and acknowledgement for that work. David Hewett's words follow, and these are the most fitting to include, without my additions, except for brief explanations of police material referred to. There may not be a biography or a memoir of Charles, but this is a detailed account of his career. It seems only fitting that this account should be added to Bert Hannam's biography, as Hewett was the most prominent of Hannam's colleagues, appearing in many of the press reports and photographs during the Bodkins Adams case, and of course also speaking in court, notably concerning the issue of the police notebooks, the use of which Lawrence attempted to scrutinise to cast some doubt on the investigation.

Early Life and Education

Hewett was born in Wokingham, Berkshire, where his father was stationed in the Berkshire Constabulary, the third generation in direct line of his family to have served in that Force. Educated at King Alfred's School (now King Alfred's Community and Sports College), Wantage, Hewett's education was interrupted at the age of sixteen when his father died in service, making it necessary for him to finish his education in order to assist his mother and sisters. They moved to Gloucestershire, where Hewett's maternal grandfather farmed.

Hewett was employed by local acquaintances the Gibbs family, who lived at Ablington Manor, near Bibury. A forebear of the family, Joseph Gibbs (cricketer), was an English first-class cricketer and the author of a book about life in the Cotswolds in the late nineteenth century. Hewett subsequently went to work at nearby Winson Manor, where he learnt to drive and trained as a chauffeur before moving to London, where he was employed by the Great Western Railway for a period.

Early Police Career

In 1937, while test-driving a Railton Straight Eight (car) for GWR at Brooklands, Hewett met a Flying Squad driver and as a result was reunited with a childhood friend, Charles Sparks. Their fathers had served together in the Berkshire Constabulary and Sparks, already serving with the Met, was able to persuade Hewett that his future lay in a police career, despite Hewett's father having once warned his son against joining the Met. At 5 feet 8 inches, his height then precluded him from becoming the fourth generation to serve in a county constabulary.

Hewett joined the Metropolitan Police on 25 April 1938. He was initially posted to 'T' Division (Hammersmith) and completed his probationary period of service on 'X' Division (Ealing) as a Temporary Detective Constable, before being posted to New Scotland Yard (the Norman Shaw Buildings) in 1945, as a Detective Constable in C.O.C4 of the Met's Criminal Investigation Department. He would remain in the CID for the rest of his career.

CID Career and Notable Investigations
The Battle of London Airport, 1948

In July 1948, Hewett was promoted to Detective Sergeant and transferred to Scotland Yard's C.O.C8, Flying Squad. Within days of his arrival, and because his appearance belied his profession, he was selected to take the part of a BOAC security guard when the squad learnt of plans to steal gold bullion and other valuables valued at £500,000 from BOAC's secure hangar at London (now Heathrow) Airport in an operation which the press termed 'The Battle of London Airport'.

A gang of professional criminals had secured the assistance of an airport employee, whose task, on the night of the raid, was to drug the coffee the security guards were routinely served. Unknown to the gang, the employee had informed the police of their plans in return for a new identity and relocation to Australia. Hewett and two fellow squad officers, dressed in BOAC security guards' uniforms, pretended to have drunk the drugged coffee when the heavily armed gang arrived in the late evening of 28 July 1948.

The officers were violently assaulted – to ensure their unconsciousness was not feigned – before the keys to the bullion safe were removed from Hewett's uniform belt. When the gang leader opened the safe, the rest of the squad, who had concealed themselves behind packing cases in the secure compound, announced their presence and a violent and prolonged melee ensued, resulting in serious injuries to both sides, before nine gang members were incapacitated and arrested.

At the outset of the affray the gang leader, Alfred Roome, struck the squad's Bob Lee over the head with a set of bolt croppers. The blow split Lee's scalp open and Hewett, observing this, believed Lee had been killed. Hewett made it his task to arrest Roome and a violent fight developed between them. Initially Hewett was on the defensive, dodging wild blows from the croppers. However, he was able to bring a packing case down on Roome, thereby disarming him, and, following a lengthy fight, during which Roome was seriously injured, the gang leader was arrested. One experienced squad officer also involved in the battle likened Hewett to 'a very angry school prefect, wiping the schoolyard with a bully with whom he had finally lost all patience'.

Subsequent forensic tests on the drugged coffee showed that it contained a quantity of barbiturate sufficient to have killed anyone drinking it many times over. They were arraigned before the Recorder of London, Sir Gerald Dodson, at the Old Bailey. It may be that Sir Gerald was aware of the amount of barbiturate used; in any event he refused to countenance their plea to a count of conspiracy to rob, an offence which at the time carried a maximum sentence of just two years' imprisonment. Eventually, all the gang pleaded to a count of robbing Detective Hewett of four keys with violence.

Counsel for Roome, whose injuries had precluded his appearing at the magistrates' court and who appeared with his co-defendants at the arraignment by virtue of a voluntary bill of indictment and an ambulance, sought to reduce what he acknowledged would be a lengthy term of imprisonment by drawing the judge's attention to the injuries his client had suffered at the hands of the police during the course of his arrest. Sir Gerald must have had in mind the passing into law of the Criminal Justice Act 1947 when he said this: 'Since Parliament has recently seen fit to pass an Act abolishing corporal punishment as a means of criminal sentence, it no longer exists in law. Strictly logically the injuries you have suffered are no punishment at all – merely part of the risk you ran. You went prepared for violence and you got it, you got the worst of it and you can hardly complain about that.' The gang received a total of seventy-one years' imprisonment.

For his part in the raid, Hewett received a Commissioner's High Commendation for 'great courage and determination in dealing with a gang of armed criminals'. Hewett's part in the affair and his future were perhaps best summed up by Bill ('the Cherub') Chapman, Bob Lee's boss and head of the squad. He invited Hewett into his office to confirm the commendation and said to him, 'Young man, if that is how you behave when in uniform then much better we keep you in the CID for as long as possible!'

In May 2004 history repeated itself when a copy-cat gang was again foiled by the Flying Squad, in an attempted robbery of gold bullion and cash on the Swissport Cargo Warehouse at Heathrow Airport.

The John Bodkin Adams Enquiry, 1956–1957
In 1954, Hewett was transferred on promotion to Scotland Yard's C.O. C1, Murder & Serious Crimes Squad, which in those days was often called in by constabularies to investigate serious crime committed in the provinces.

In 1956, with Detective Superintendent Herbert Hannam, Hewett was called in by the Chief Constable of Eastbourne Borough police to take over the investigation of the activities of suspected serial killer John Bodkin Adams in Eastbourne. The investigation and trial became a *cause celebre*, the subject of intense national and international press interest.

Following months of investigation, a report was submitted to the Director of Public Prosecutions. Because poisoning was alleged and the court proceedings commenced prior to the Homicide Act 1957 coming into force, the offence carried capital punishment, and so it was required that the Attorney General for England and Wales conduct the prosecution. The advice of the then Attorney General, Sir Reginald Manningham-Buller, was therefore sought at an early stage and Hannam and Hewett were astounded when he advised Adams should first face trial for murdering a single victim (Edith Alice Morrell), whose body had been cremated, thereby depriving the prosecution of valuable forensic evidence, which existed in other cases where bodies had been exhumed and toxicity tests conducted. A second indictment, alleging the murder of Gertrude Hullett, was held in reserve, to be preferred at a subsequent trial. There is considerable evidence to suggest that the trial was 'interfered with' by those 'at the highest level'. Notably, during the committal hearing for Adams in January 1957, the Lord Chief Justice, Rayner Goddard was seen dining with the defendant's suspected lover, Sir Roland Gwynne (Chairman of the local Magistrates' Bench and Mayor of Eastbourne from 1929 to 1931), and ex-Attorney-General Hartley Shawcross at a hotel in Lewes. This is all speculation, but it adds interest.

The trial, which had to be transferred from Lewes Assizes to the Old Bailey to ensure a fair hearing, was described at the time as 'one of the greatest murder trials of all time' and 'the murder trial of the twentieth century'. At the time of the trial, it was only possible to include one count of murder on a single indictment. This, together with the problem of proving murder in respect of one whose duty was to relieve the suffering of an individual with a terminal disease, added to the prosecution's difficulties. The Attorney General's confidence that he could cross-examine Adams thoroughly, was confounded when the opposition opted not to call the defendant to give evidence.

After what was then the longest murder trial in British history, seventeen days, the jury took just forty-five minutes to acquit the accused. At the conclusion of the proceedings the Attorney General shocked the detectives and the trial judge, Patrick Devlin, by announcing his intention to enter a *nolle prosequi*, staying all further murder proceedings against Adams. The Attorney General's action was considered by Devlin in his post-trial book to be 'an abuse of process'. It led Hewett to question Manningham-Buller's partiality in his conduct of the case, suspecting he had succumbed to political interference.

Although disappointed at the outcome, Hewett was philosophical, recognising the considerable evidence of a concerted effort by senior members of the medical, legal, judicial and political professions to avoid Adams' being convicted. Hewett said afterwards that the failure of the case against Adams was also the result of the considerable delay which occurred prior to the Yard being called in, making a successful investigation more difficult. He always maintained that Adams was a serial killer but that it would have been more advisable to have charged him with the manslaughter rather than with the murder of his patients, given the relative lack of understanding of the motives of serial killers at the time.

It is worthy of note that Scotland Yard's files on the case and those of the prosecution were initially ordered to be closed to public view for an extended period of seventy-five years, meaning they were closed until 2033. This appears an unjustifiable decision, considering the advanced age of the suspect, witnesses and others involved in the case. In fact, the files were opened to the public after special permission was finally granted in 2003, following the Dr Harold Shipman case and Hewett's death in March that year.

The Black Mountains Lime Fraud, 1959–1962
In 1958 Hewett was promoted to Detective Inspector and transferred to Scotland Yard's C.O. C6, Fraud Squad. In January 1959, he was

called in at the request of the Chief Constable of Carmarthen and Cardigan, following initial enquiries by the Investigation Branch of the then Ministry of Agriculture, Fisheries and Food, to investigate a major fraud in Carmarthen, Wales, which became known as the 'West Wales Lime fraud enquiry'.

With the assistance of Welsh-speaking colleagues Gwyn Waters and Clifford Turvey, as well as local constabulary officers, Hewett carried out a detailed investigation, lasting over two years. The enquiry uncovered a massive conspiracy involving a Welsh Co-operative Society, several of the society's officers and operatives, local mine and quarry owners and in excess of 1,400 local farmers, who defrauded the Ministry by claiming the lime subsidy in respect of deliveries, which were either overestimated, never made or, in fact, deliveries of coal.

The annual cost of the subsidy at the time was approximately £10 million and it was suspected that the Ministry had been defrauded of an amount exceeding £1 million over a nine-year period (£21 million at 2014 values). However, to keep the criminal investigation and any subsequent proceedings within reasonable bounds Hewett concentrated on just the most recent three-year period. Even so, the committal proceedings occupied thirty-two days of court time, and the trial, at Carmarthen Assizes in 1962, took fifty-five days; at the time the longest UK criminal trial of the twentieth century.

All the defendants were convicted and sentenced to terms of imprisonment and at the conclusion of the proceedings, the judge, Sir Alan Mocatta QC, described the case as being not only one of the lengthiest but also one of the most complex investigations ever to come before a court. He commended the officers, who were also commended by the Director of Public Prosecutions and the Metropolitan Police Commissioner.

The Mitcham Co-op Depot murder, 1962

In 1962, while a detective chief inspector on the Met's 'W' Division at Tooting, Hewett led the investigation into a raid on the Mitcham Co-operative Society's depot on 17 November. During the course of the robbery, Dennis Hurden, a thirty-five-year-old Co-op lorry driver and father of two, unaware of the raid, made his way to his vehicle to begin his day's work and was gratuitously shot and killed by George Thatcher, one of the four robbers.

What made the case unique and difficult to detect was that Thatcher was at the time serving a seven-year sentence in HMP Dartmoor for a previous offence of armed robbery. On the face of it, therefore, he could not have participated in the crime, although it was one for which his criminal record and *modus operandi* would otherwise have made him a suspect. It was only following intensive police enquiries that it was uncovered that, *without police having being informed*, Thatcher had been given a release licence from Dartmoor by the Home Office, allowing him freedom during the day as long as he returned to a hostel, at Pentonville, at night. Armed with this information, Hewett's team was able to establish Thatcher's participation and to identify his fellow robbers.

The gang members pleaded not guilty to the murder charge but were all convicted by an Old Bailey jury. The trial judge, Eustace Roskill, described the gang as 'one of the most dangerous ever to be brought to justice'. Passing the death sentence on Thatcher, the judge said, 'You shot Dennis Hurden brutally and without reason or pity. The law prescribes but one sentence, that you too shall die.' The other three, Philip Kelly, John Hilton and Charles Connelly, were sentenced to life imprisonment. Thatcher's conviction was confirmed following an appeal but, as was becoming increasingly common at that time, the death sentence was commuted to life imprisonment.

It is worthy of note that within a month of Hilton's release from prison on licence in January 1978, after serving sixteen years of his life sentence, he participated in a robbery on a jeweller's in Golder's Green, during the course of which Hilton shot both the jeweller, Leo Grunhut, and his fellow robber, Alan Roberts. The jeweller died immediately but Roberts did not. Hilton took Roberts to a lock-up garage and tried to treat his gunshot wound. He did not take Roberts to hospital because he knew that, if he did, he would probably be apprehended and face conviction for the armed robbery and the murder of Mr Grunhut. Instead, Hilton allowed Mr Roberts to bleed to death in the lock-up garage. He then buried the body on a railway embankment in Kent.

Hilton was not apprehended immediately and his involvement only came to light in 1991, following his arrest for yet another robbery during which he used a gun, when he admitted shooting Grunhut and Roberts. On this occasion he was given a whole life sentence but this was reduced on appeal to a sentence of twenty-five years in 2008 because of the progress he had made in prison in the intervening seventeen years.

The Dulwich Picture Gallery Theft, 1966

While Detective Superintendent of the Met's 'M' Division (Southwark), Hewett was in charge of an area of central London that was a principal battleground between the South London Richardson Gang and the Kray Twins, based in the East End of London.

On 31 December 1966, with eleven murders at various stages of investigation or prosecution, and with his annual crime report almost completed, Hewett was informed that eight paintings had been stolen from the Dulwich Picture Gallery. They were estimated to be worth at least £3 million at the time, making this the UK's biggest robbery, exceeding the amount stolen in the 1963 Great Train Robbery.

Initial investigation suggested the raid had been meticulously planned and executed so as to circumvent the security system, and there were immediate fears that the paintings would be smuggled abroad. Initially a reward of just £1,000 was offered on behalf of the gallery by its chairman, Hartley Shawcross, though this was later increased to £5,000. When Hewett learnt of Shawcross's connection with the case he contacted the commissioner to explain his concerns in the light of Shawcross's apparent involvement in the Bodkin Adams' enquiry. The commissioner approached the then Attorney-General, Lord Elwyn-Jones, who allegedly discussed the matter with Shawcross and obtained his undertaking that he would have no further personal involvement of any kind in the enquiry.

Hewett decided that maximum publicity about the paintings stolen would reduce the risk of them being concealed successfully and he made substantial use of both the press and television media to alert the public to the crime and his investigation. Local door-to-door enquiries produced some evidence of a Ford Corsair pulling away from Gallery Road at the time of the theft; the vehicle was identified and, within a couple of days, found, abandoned, with tools and traces which were forensically linked to the crime. Hewett kept these developments on the front page and on news broadcasts, in the hope this would crack the thieves' nerve. This hope appears to have been borne out because within hours information was received that led Hewett to recover three of the paintings from a West Kensington flat. However, at this stage Hewett consulted with the commissioner and formally ordered paper editors not to publish this news, feeling the silence would encourage the return of the other paintings, and within twenty-four hours an anonymous call led Hewett's team to where the remaining paintings had been abandoned on Streatham Common.

On the wrappings round the paintings a stray fingerprint was found, which matched those of one Michael Hall, a man with a record of offences for petty theft, who was living nearby, at West Norwood. He was arrested and confessed, claiming to have acted alone, although Hewett believed he must have had at least two accomplices. Hall was charged with the theft of the pictures, together with five other unconnected offences of receiving stolen goods. He pleaded guilty at the Central Criminal Court and was sentenced to five years' imprisonment.

Sir Carl Aarvold, the Recorder of London, commended the investigating officers on the recovery of all of the paintings in such a short time and the arrest of even one of those involved in their theft, something rare in major picture thefts.

Retirement

In May 1968, having delayed his retirement, following the sudden death of the then Metropolitan Police Commissioner, Joseph Simpson, in March that year, Hewett retired from the Met with an exemplary Certificate of Conduct and a total of twenty-nine Commissioner's, Judges' and DPP's Commendations. He took up an appointment as security consultant with the Wates Group and became a regular speaker on behalf of the Home Office, the National Federation of Builders and the National House Building Council on security issues in the construction industry.

Appendix 3

CORNER SHOP MURDERS

The Emily Pye murder highlights a prominent feature of the violent crime in the 1950s, and that is the prevalence of attacks on corner shops. The vulnerability of these premises is obvious, and in the post-war years there were gangs and plenty of wartime weapons. Combine the two and you have major potential for terrifying robberies and violence. Emily Pye was killed for a meagre sum of money, as it turned out. In a survey of criminal homicide in England between 1957 and 1962, Terence Morris and Louis Blom-Cooper listed a large number of such attacks and violent robberies, and as a typical example of what tended to happen, we have this:

> During the course of a burgling of a co-op store, Jones (38) a moulder, heard the manager (38) returning, presumably to lock up the office safe, which had been left open. As he came up the stairs, Jones hit him once and hurried away, taking £76 and 30,000 cigarettes. Turner died immediately from a fractured skull.[123]

More typically, though, the victim was female, as with Emily. In 1949 we have two of the first examples of such a murder. Both are still unsolved. First there was Emily Armstrong, beaten to death in a drycleaner's shop in London. Then there is Gertude O'Leary, sixty-six, a licensee, violently murdered, in Bristol. Of course, there were plenty of attacks on old ladies in their homes too, as with the unsolved 1956 killing of two sisters in Asmall Lane, Merseyside. The case clearly resembles Emily's.

In Halifax, Hannam was up against the problem of a high population density, clustered in several red-brick streets around the Gibbet Street shop, and other circumstances from weather to the bank holiday, complicated tracing efforts and investigations into individual movements and sightings.

The chronicle of such killings of vulnerable people over the period of Hannam's life in the police is astonishingly long and depressing. I collected a list of unsolved cases in Yorkshire between 1938 and 1966, and this list is interesting when compared to the Pye murder:

1938: Body of Margaret Peel found in the room behind her shop at Fewston, between Harrogate and Skipton. Her husband was charged but acquitted.

1945: Body of Annie Nichols found in her shop in Bramley, Leeds.

1948: Henry Warner found on the floor of his shop in Wellington Street, Leeds. He died without being able to speak and give information.

1955: Frances Hodgson found dead in her shop at Bradford.

1957: Emily Pye murder.

1966: Fred Craven, bookmaker, killed in his shop at Bingley.

1966: Winifred Sharp found shot dead at the post office in Leeds.

These are just the unsolved murder cases. In addition, there are dozens of attacks on shop owners and assistants in the record. One would have thought that a special squad for protection of such places would have been formed, and surely one would expect special interest in the Pye case due to the Frances Hodgson case just two years before, and in nearby Bradford. In that particular area, over a period of forty years, there have been thirty unsolved murders.

Appendix 4

EASTBOURNE

Among the many footnotes to the Bodkin Adams case, there is the interesting matter of the seaside town as Adams knew it, and particularly of the two very different parts of the place, as described by Pamela Cullen, who lived in the town when she wrote her exhaustive account of the investigations and trial. She wrote, 'It transformed itself into a coastal spa without the tackiness which often attends such places ... People with wealth and influence had settled in large mansions to the west of the town; they and the hotels found their staff in the meaner streets on the east side.'[124]

The nature of this division in the town is clearly shown in the feature in the French magazine *Detective*, with its picture of Gertrude Hullett's house. It faces the sea, with Beachy Head close by and a playing field right outside the garden room at the front. Down the side runs a quiet road, along which stands a tall wooden fence. But people walk around right outside the property; over the other side, very close again to the house, is an extensive area of more large homes. The magazine calls this 'the most aristocratic quarter of Eastbourne', and so it is, but the ordinary folk play and stroll very close by. Adams' visits would have been open to view; passers-by would have been aware of him, arriving in his flashy car.

As with most typical English seaside towns, there are memories such as this, with a touch of the Madame Tussaud excitement: 'The pier was a magical place and had penny slot machines which depicted scenes of hanging and graveyards with skeletons coming out of the grounds. This obviously passed for entertainment in the 1950s...'[125] But although there was plenty of day-tripper proletarian fun that George Orwell would have appreciated in his documentary mode, memories such as this do show very clearly the two microcosms within the town. Adams preferred his wealthy patients, but everything was quite bunched together really. His own place, Kent Lodge, was impressive, but the other Eastbourne was a short walk away. Adams knew the place well, and would have seen lots of it during the terrible bombing of 1941–42, when it experienced ninety-eight German attacks.

Pamela Cullen gives a very detailed picture of the town she knows, and it is easy to imagine from her account that Adams would have been a very familiar figure there; after all, he was a distinctive figure, very large, rotund and a real presence. Some contemporary photographs capture this, as in one shot in which a mother and her child stop to stare at him as he walks by, sturdy, aloof and rather coldly, as if striding through some alien place and needing to arrive somewhere more comfortable.

Hannam knew the place well, and he was there so long that he regularly met his team in a pub to talk over the day's work. There is a sense, when one reads between the lines, that he soon understood that he had to push things a little in order to get a response, so set in its ways was the place. The entire Adams saga is embedded in the doctor's own 'patch' and his comfortable routine. Hannam saw this, and it is almost certainly the case that his 'chance meeting' was a definite ploy – a gambit – as he was on the suspect's own 'turf' and felt an unorthodox move was essential.

What the Eastbourne context shows us more than anything is the centrality of class identity at the time. David Kynaston, in his sweeping survey of the years 1951 to 1957, notes:

> Audience research revealed in 1950 that only 25 per cent of viewers with incomes of more than £1,000 approved of music-hall programmes, against 65 per cent of viewers with incomes less than £350; as for listening habits, BBC figures in 1947 showed that on a typical evening, the Third Programme was heard at some point by 24 per cent of the upper middle class, 12 per cent of the lower middle class and only 3 per cent of the working class.[126]

Bodkin Adams was openly courting and cultivating the upper echelons of society. In a town which reached the pages of *The Times* mostly for bridge, croquet and cricket – along with summer temperatures, of course – Adams was in the perfect milieu to cling to the culture of dinner parties and afternoon tea. But as regards the legacy of the affair (a word he would have liked), it is interesting to note that Adams features in a popular reference work called *Crimes and Criminals*, with a photograph, though of course his only listed crimes are fairly minor frauds. That irony would have amused Bert Hannam.[127]

NOTES AND REFERENCES

N.B. The references to material conveyed by Iain Hannam, Herbert's grandson, and by other workmates and peers of Herbert, are from e-mails or from telephone conversations with the author. This all took place between November 2017 and January 2018.

Abbreviations used:
'Hoskins' refers to *Two Men Were Acquitted* unless other titles are specified.
'Cullen' refers to *A Stranger in Blood*.

  1 Letter from the author's collection
  2 *Report on Detective Work and Procedure* Vol. II p. 9
  3 Hoskins p. 17
  4 ibid. p. 18
  5 See Fido and Skinner p. 269
  6 Simpson, Keith, *Forty Years of Murder* p. 27
  7 ibid. p. 29
  8 ibid. p. 93
  9 Lefebure, Molly, *Murder on the Home Front* p. 179
 10 Wade, Stephen, *Lincolnshire Murders* p. 71
 11 Lefebure p.192
 12 Cecil, Henry, *The Trial of Walter Rowland* p. 49
 13 ibid. p. 56

14 Paget p. 40

15 Paget p. 70

16 [?]

17 *Exchange Control Committee Report 1915–1939* p. 274

18 ibid. p. 275

19 ibid. p. 278

20 ibid. p. 289. For a very useful explanation of the problems linked to the gold standard and to currency controvertibility, see Glasner, David, 'Where Keynes Went Wrong' in *Encounter* December 1988, pp. 57–65. He offers this explanation for lay readers: 'Before the First World War five French francs were worth about one dollar. If it cost fewer than five times as many francs to buy wheat in Paris as it cost dollars to buy wheat in Chicago, one would profitably convert dollars into their equivalent in francs and buy the wheat in Paris instead of in Chicago ... Because the same possibility existed for all internationally traded commodities, prices in all Gold Standard countries could not deviate from a common level.' Britain, of course, had abandoned the gold standard in 1925.

21 *The Exchange Control Act 1947* Ch. 14 p. 1

22 See Bryant, Arthur, 'Our Notebook', *Illustrated London News* 11 September 1948 p. 282. This was written in the context of yet another royal wedding, after Queen Elizabeth II's the previous year.

23 See advert for Johnnie Walker whisky, ibid, back page

24 'Clothes Coupons May Have to Last Longer', *Daily Mail* 21 August 1945 p. 5

25 *Exchange Control Act* Ch. 14 p. 2

26 'Yard Man to Probe Dollar Rackets' *Evening Telegraph and Post* 16 August 1947 p. 3

27 See 'Anglo-American Film Agreement' *The Times* 11 July 1938 p. 4

28 See the full discussion on Hansard 17 June 1948 Vol. 542 pp. 737–78

29 ibid. p.3/19 online edition

30 'Super-Snooping' *Courier and Advertiser* 24 September 1947 p. 2

31 Priestley, J. B., *Delight* p. 17

32 See Wingersky, Melvin, 'Report of the Royal Commission on Capital Punishment (1949-1953): A Review' in *Journal of Criminal Law and Criminology* Vol. 44, Issue 6 p. 22 In this context, it

is interesting to note the remarks made by a prominent public prosecutor writing in a work published at this time: 'I am a great admirer of the police in this country... they have up against them daily the most evil men and the worst liars imaginable... You can't fight such men in kid gloves but you can always be fair...' But he adds to the hanging debate a reference to Timothy Evans, hanged (wrongly as we now know) close to the time of the Adams trial, 'Can you go to bed at night to sleep with the certainty that Timothy Evans was rightly convicted and hanged? I can't.' (*I Was a Public Prosecutor* p.163)

33 *Daily Mail* 2 June 1953 p. 2

34 *News Chronicle* 28 October 1953 p. 4

35 Fraser, Frankie, *Mad Frank's Britain*

36 Morton, James, 'Murder Most Foul' *Law Society Gazette* 3 June 2005 pp. 1–2

37 *The News Chronicle* 29 October 1953 p. 6

38 Fraser, Frankie, *Mad Frank's Britain*

39 The relevant *Times* reports are a 'Former detective says he Confused two Letters' and 'Allegations Denied by the Attorney General' on 10 November 1973 and 12 November 1973 respectively.

40 See 'Lack of Police in London' *Times Digital Archive* 29 September 1951

41 Clerk, Carol, *Getting it Straight* p. 40

42 See Old Police Cells Museum: 'The Brighton Police Corruption Case' at www.oldpolicecellsmuseum.org.uk

43 See Thomas, Donald, *Villain's Paradise* p. 428

44 Browne, Douglas G., *The Rise of Scotland Yard*

45 Hoskins, *Two Men Were Acquitted* p. 68

46 See Cullen p. 189

47 Brown, Alyson, 'Britain's Bonnie and Clyde' *BBC History Magazine* December 2017 p. 62

48 Hoskins p. 122

49 ibid.

50 ibid.

51 'Confidences to Doctors' *The Times* 5 October 1948 p. 2

52 Atkinson, Tony, *A Prescribed Life* p. 35

53 Hoskins p. 42

54 ibid. p. 43

55 Evelyn, Michael, 'Mathew, Sir Theobald' ODNB online p. 2. The Medical Defence Union, in its advertising for practitioners, demanded an entrance fee of 10 shillings, followed by an annual subscription of £1. Its relevant aim was 'to advise and defend or assist in defending Members of the Union in cases where proceedings involving questions of professional principle or otherwise are brought against them'. It was a very reasonable outlay for such protection in law.

56 Cullen, p. 271 Note: I had to consider the real meaning of this, as the text in Cullen's book has 'seems to abundant...' The typo, in my view, relates to 'so abundant' which makes more sense.

57 ibid. p.272

58 ibid. p.275

59 Jackson, Stanley, *The Old Bailey* p. 196

60 *The Medical Annual* 1923 p. 144 Incidentally, it is worth commenting also, bearing in mind Dr Adams' penchant for flashy cars, that the same volume recommends the 'All British Standard Light Car' which is 'always ready for service and requires a minimum of attention'.

61 Special Correspondent, 'Trial of Dr. J. Bodkin Adams' *British Medical Journal* 6 April 1957 p. 1

62 See Hoskins pp. 125-126. It is notable that Hoskins provides a personal, very biased commentary on the interaction between Hannam and Lawrence, when in fact, nothing else suggests the kind of acrimony he detects. It was more likely a meeting of minds, and Hannam was too smart to budge when many would have done. It is plain to see that Lawrence could bully and coerce, as he had patently done with the nurses in the opening days of the trial.

63 Hoskins p. 127

64 ibid. p. 127–128

65 Special Correspondent, 'Trial of Dr. J. Bodkin Adams' *British Medical Journal* 6 April, 1957

66 Hoskins, p. 181

67 ibid. p.183

68 ibid. p. 203

69 'Doctor John Bodkin Adams' *Women's Lives, Women's Voices 1947-1957* p. 24

70 Interview with Jane Robins

71 See Devlin, Patrick, *Easing the Passing*

72 See the French *Detective* magazine, 3 September 1956 p. 4. The feature manages to use photos which were not seen in the British press, and for the French publication, Hannam is the giant of the whole case; they blow up the image of him walking in Eastbourne to dominate the main page of reportage. The only image which is larger is, of course, that of Bodkin Adams.

73 'Sergeant tells of talk in gaol room' *News Chronicle* 29 October 1953

74 Wilkes, Roger, 'Inside Story: Kent Lodge' *Daily Telegraph* 3 March 2001 p. 3

75 See 'Widespread Appeal for Condemned Mother'. On the other hand, in contrast to the serious aspect of a murder charge, there was the case W. J. A. Grant, a magistrate of Hillerdon, near Exeter, who wanted to die and put on a 'swan dance' of farewell for friends, as a farewell to life (*Courier and Advertiser* 23 August 1954 p. 4).

76 See Wade, Stephen, *Heroes, Villains and Victims of Leeds* pp. 92–96

77 'Right to Die Movement' *Aberdeen Press and Journal* 26 October 1935 p. 7

78 'Lord Horder and the Right to Die' *The Western Daily Press* 13 December 1935

79 'Brutal Murder of Woman Aged 80' *The Times* 27 September 1957 p. 7

80 See Belinda Webb-Blofeld review of 'The Littlehampton Libels' *The Times Literary Supplement* 5 January 2018 p. 30

81 See 'The Halifax Slasher' www.2ubh.com/slasher/ referring to a film being made on the case by Barry Kavanagh. The *Halifax Courier* also carries several features on the case.

82 See 'Search for Killer of Woman Shopkeeper' *Halifax Courier* 29 September, 1957 p. 2

83 ibid.

84 'Life and Death of Poor Emily' *Halifax Courier* 12 June 2007, online

85 See 'Unending Mystery of who Killed Emily Pye' *Halifax Courier* 28 June 2017 online, referring to a letter from David Glover, which gave details of Emily's earlier life.

86 See Southworth, Louis, 'Police Dogs' in Morland, Nigel, *Crime and Detection* pp. 65–70

87 See material on the Desborough Committee in *The Encyclopedia of Scotland Yard* p. 67. 'Its generous pay settlement was anticipated by an immediate payment of £10, which undermined the police strike, 1919.'

88 Letter to *The Times* 12 September 1909
89 For the beginnings of the Police federation see [address].
90 Clunn, Harold P., *The Face of London* p. 384
91 'Police Education' *Aberdeen Press and Journal* 12 October 1927 p. 4
92 See the interesting profile of Hannam in Jane Robins' book, *The Curious Habits of Dr Adams*
93 Cullen, Pamela, *A Stranger in Blood* p. 41
94 Letter in the author's possession.
95 Goddard, Lesley, 'From Police Cadet to Police Officer' *Spectrum* special issue
96 Hoskins p. 217
97 ibid. p. 126
98 Pierrepoint, Albert, *Executioner: Pierrepoint*
99 See 'What Hendon Did for the Police' *The Times* 7 May 1959 p. 13. This feature gives a very useful summary of the changes in police training between 1948 and 1959.
100 ibid. p. 13
101 Trenchard, Lord, 'Leadership in the Police' *The Times* 26 March 1947 p. 5
102 This is quoted in chapter 2, but this is the text again: 'Dear Bert, Many thanks for the loan ... I think your comments on the various pages are well merited. They show clearly the difference between learning the fact and commenting on it by what one reads...'
103 See Nixon, D. H. C., *Nick of the River* p. 24
104 *Report on Detective Work and Procedure* p. 99
105 Simpson, Keith, *Forty Years of Murder* p. 209
106 Fraser, Frankie, *Mad Frank's Britain* p. 39
107 See the profile of Hoskins in *No Hiding Place* p. 4
108 Cullen p. 46
109 ibid. p. 45
110 ibid. p. 46
111 See D'Cruze, Shani, *et al.*, *Murder*
112 Macilwee, Michael, *The Teddy Boy Wars* p. 257
113 Cherrill, Fred, *Cherrill of the Yard* p. 255
114 *The Youth's Instructor and Guardian* p. 302
115 Author's notes on an oral history project done as a school project 1977

116 Notes from a nurse's notebook in the author's possession.

117 Mahar, Caitlin, 'R v Adams and Terminal Care in Postwar Britain' p. 163

118 ibid p. 165

119 Hoyle, Clifford, 'The Care of the Dying', *Post-Graduate Medical Journal* April 1944 p. 123

120. *Black's Medical Dictionary* p. 462.

121 *Real Life Crimes* 1 p. 22

122 'Doctors Bar Mercy Killing' *Gloucestershire Echo* 18 October 1950 p. 1

123 Morris, Terence, and Blom-Cooper, Louis, *A Calendar of Murder* p. 57

124 Cullen p. 26

125 See www.eastbourneherald.co.uk, 'Nostalgia – Eastbourne memories'

126 Kynaston, David, *Family Britain 1951-1957* p. 137

127 Vandome, Nick, *Crime and Criminals* pp. 5-6. Vandome wrote: 'Although there was no proof to suggest that Adams was murdering his patients there was strong circumstantial evidence. He frequently telephoned solicitors and asked them to come immediately to witness the signing of a new will in his favour.' This is exactly the kind of background note to the investigation which led Hannam to follow the by-ways as well as the highways of enquiry. The result is patently that Adams sits alongside so many notorious killers in the reference works. Also, in William Donaldson's *Rogues, Villains and Eccentrics*, Adams is there again, and the author gives a similarly cautious assessment, ending with '... most students of the case believe that he dispatched at least nine elderly ladies for personal gain.'

BIBLIOGRAPHY AND SOURCES

A Bibliographical Survey

As police literature in true crime has a limited scope, some help here on the extent and nature of the genre will prove helpful to readers wishing to know more. Engaging in research in this area, one soon discovers that the meatiest material is generally found in the second-hand out-of-print stocks of specialist libraries or booksellers. In Hannam's case, without the related ephemera, the already obscure would have fallen to the category of invisible. What follows is a general survey with the addition of a bibliography in particular of the Bodkin Adams case, as that has attracted most attention from a number of writers.

Hannam's involvement with the Adams and Whiteway cases has led to his being more than a footnote in the history of murder since the war. There is a considerable library on the two cases, and for the Adams sources, Pamela Cullen's book was a landmark because she was the first historian to have access to all the police files. In her book we learn the minutiae of the Hannam investigations, as the reader will see from my examples in chapter 9.

There have been numerous books devoted to the cases recounted in the foregoing pages, but the majority concern the Bodkin Adams case. There is no doubt that the most detailed and rigorous volume in this respect is *A Stranger in Blood* by Pamela V. Cullen. The author studied all the relevant archives, and she knows Eastbourne extremely well. Although the book is impressively thorough and includes a large number of relevant topics, along with tantalising speculations, there is no fluent narrative, held together by a story spine, tightly focused on the mainstream events. This has been provided recently by Jane Robins in *The Curious Habits of Dr Adams: A 1950s Murder Mystery.*

Published very close to the time of the trial are *The Trial of Dr Adams* by Sybille Bedford, who was present at the trial, and Rodney Hallworth's *Where There's a Will: The Sensational Life of Dr John Bodkin Adams.* For the reflections of the presiding judge – an extremely rare kind of publication – we have Patrick Devlin's *Easing the Passing.* Sybille Bedford followed on from her first book with *The Best We Can Do?*, published in 1989. Rob Normey, in 2016, wrote, 'In 1957 Sybille Bedford took it upon herself to attend every day of the trail and the Old Bailey and provide for her readers an hour by hour account.' Pamela Cullen's book also does virtually the same.

More recently, there have been full accounts of the affair, first from John Surtees in his *The Strange Case of Dr Bodkin Adams: The life and murder trial of Eastbourne's infamous doctor.* Of all the general accounts, the aforementioned book by Jane Robins is highly recommended. Robins helpfully lists the main suspected victims, with useful profiles. She also provides a profile of Hannam.

Most of the general works on the Adams case contain an assessment of Hannam's role, and they stress his statements made in court. There are a number of varying verdicts on what he said, but in the end we have to recall some words spoken to him by Adams in an interview: 'Murder? I did not think they could prove that.' The ambiguity of Hannam's encounters with Adams has been one major factor in the fact that the library of studies and reassessments has grown so prodigiously.

Interest has been largely in the cases themselves, but what is of particular relevance to the present work is the growth of interest in detectives and their lives in recent years; this has been a body of writing which is different from the 'true crime red and black' genre. The popular true crime gangland and villain memoirs and autobiographies tend to offer unsubstantiated material which has been handed down in anecdotal form. The tendency to assume that 'all coppers are bent' has also fed the companion literature written by popular social historians. My own earlier work is not entirely free of this either. But the recent books from Cullen and Robins have added real depth to the records. It could be argued that the most influential literature on the case has been in the mass-market crime magazines which have been produced since the 1970s in various guises, and these tend to continue the same sensationalist bias which I have identified in the French magazine, *Detective*.

If the bibliographical record on Hannam has been one-sided, then the fault is not with the media themselves, but rather with the detective's reluctance to court attention. But the popular magazine press has been just as active, and has placed Adams beside the notorious serial killers and cannibals. *Murder in Mind*, *Real Life Crimes*, *Murder Casebook* and *Unsolved Magazine* all in their different ways either accept the serial killing or ask the puzzling questions. Popular culture wishes to preserve and utilise the engrossing ambiguity of this case.

On Hannam himself there is nothing specific; in other memoirs there is material but only in slight reference, with the exception of Molly Lefebure's book on wartime crime. A trend in publishing is discernible here regarding police books; the autobiographies tend to be self-published, and many of the books published traditionally are merely histories of particular constabularies. The starting point for anyone wishing to go further in police biography is through the Police History Society, who publish monographs and have a regular journal (www.policehistorysociety.co.uk).

Annoyingly, most of the detailed material on London crime for the period of Hannam's life is in the form of what might loosely be called villains' memoirs. These may include hearsay and tall tales or lengthy explanations of social history seen 'from the bottom up' as it were.

Books Cited

Anon., *Detective Tales* (London: Atlas Publishing, 1955)

Anon., *The Youth's Instructor and Guardian* (London: J. Mason, 1834)

Atkinson, Tony, with Smailes, Lynn, *A Prescribed Life* (Melbourne: Affirm Press, 2016)

Cecil, Henry, *The Trial of Walter Rowland* (London: David and Charles, 1975)

Cherrill, Fred, *Cherrill of the Yard* (London: Odhams, 1940)

Clerk, Carol, *Getting it Straight: Villains Talking* (London: Pan Macmillan, 2008)

Clunn, Harold P., *The Face of London* (London: Simpkin Marshall Ltd, 1932)

Comrie, John D., *Black's Medical Dictionary* (London: Waverley Book Company, 1934)

Cullen, Pamela V., *A Stranger in Blood* (London: Elliott and Thompson, n.d.)

D'Cruze, Shani, Walklate, Sandra & Pegg, Samantha, *Murder* (Cullompton: Willan Publishing, 2006)

Dernley, Syd, *Memoirs of a Public Executioner* (London: Pan Books, 1990)

Devlin, Patrick, *Easing the Passing* (Faber and Faber, 1986)

Eddlestone, John J., *The Encyclopaedia of Executions* (London: John Blake, 2002)

Ensor, David, *I Was a Public Prosecutor* (London: Robert Hale, 1958)

Fido, Martin, and Skinner, Keith, *The Official Encyclopaedia of Scotland Yard* (London: Virgin Books, 1999)

Hale, Leslie, *Hanged in Error* (London: Penguin Books, 1961)

Hoskins, Percy, *Two Men Were Acquitted* (London: Secker and Warburg, 1984)

Jackson, Stanley, *The Old Bailey* (London: W. H. Allen, 1978)

Koestler, Arthur & Rolph, C. H., *Hanged by the Neck* (London: Penguin Books, 1961)

Lefebure, Molly, *Murder on the Home Front* (London: Sphere, 2013)

McLaughlin, Stewart, *Harry Allen: Britain's Last Hangman* (London: True Crime Library, 2008)

Macilwee, Michael, *The Teddy Boy Wars* (Croydon: Milo Books, 2015)

Marwick, Arthur, *British Society since 1945* (London: Penguin, 1982)

Morland, Nigel (ed.), *Crime and Detection* (Oxford: Tallis Press, 1966)

Paget, R. T. *et al.*, *Hanged – and Innocent?* (London: Victor Gollancz, 1953)

Pierrepoint, Albert, *Executioner: Pierrepoint* (London: Hodder and Stoughton, 1974)

Priestley, J. B., *Delight* (London: Heinemann, 1949)

Richardson, Anthony, *Nick of the River* (London: George Harrap, 1955)

Robins, Jane, *The Curious Habits of Dr Adams: A 1950s Murder Mystery* (London: John Murray, 2013)

Simpson, Keith, *Forty Years of Murder* (London: Harrap, 1978)

Thomas, Donald, *Villain's Paradise* (London: John Murray, 2005)

Wade, Stephen, *Lincolnshire Murders* (Stroud: The History Press, 2006)

Young, Hugh, *My Forty Years at the Yard* (London: W. H. Allen, 1955)

Other Works Cited

Anon., 'Doctor John Bodkin Adams: Good or Bad?' *Women's Lives, Women's Voices 1947-1957* Intergenerational history project (Eastbourne: East Sussex County Council, 2016)

Goddard, Lesley, 'From Police Cadet to Police Officer' Metropolitan Police, Cadet Corps issue of *Spectrum* souvenir brochure (London: *Spectrum Magazine*, 1981)

Articles in Periodicals and Newspapers/Online & Print

Anon., *News Chronicle* 28–29 October 1953 pp. 4 & 6

Anon., 'That's the way to do it! Kids pay to see justice done' *New Scientist* Dec. 2017 p. 17

Anon., 'The British Film Import Duty 1947-48' [www.terramedia.co.uk/reference/law/british]

Anon., 'The Rural School' *The Countryman* April–June 1941 pp. 19–27

Anon. (special correspondent), 'Trial of Doctor J. Bodkin Adams' *The British Medical Journal* (London: BMJ, 1957) pp. 828–836

Anon., 'Un Fantastique Tueur de Dames' *Detective* 3 September 1956 pp. 3–5

Brown, Alyson, 'Britain's Bonnie and Clyde' *BBC History Magazine* Dec. 2017 pp. 60–64

Bryant, Arthur, 'Our Notebook' *The Illustrated London News* 22 Nov. 1947 p. 562

Bryant, Arthur, 'Our Notebook' *The Illustrated London News* 11 Sept. 1948 p. 282

Anon., 'Centenary Countdown' *Narpo News* Issue 91 August 2017 p. 14

Evelyn, Michael, 'Mathew, Sir Theobald' *Oxford Dictionary of National Biography* [https://doi.org/10.1093/ref:odnb/34932]

Fido, Martin, 'Doctor Death' *Real Life Crimes* 1 (London: Eaglemoss Publications 2002)

Glasner, David, 'Where Keynes Went Wrong' *Encounter* December 1988 pp. 57–65

Mahar, Caitlin, 'Easing the Passing: R v Adams and Terminal Care in Postwar Britain' *Social History of Medicine* Vol. 28 No. 1 pp. 155–171

Mark, Robert, 'The High Cost of Hanging' *Crime and Detection* (Oxford: Tallis Press, 1966) pp. 7–15

Thompson, Ian, 'Down and Out in Bombay and London' *Times Literary Supplement* 22–29 December 2017 p. 17

Webb-Blofeld, Belinda, 'Review of The Littlehampton Libels' *Times Literary Supplement* 5 January 2017 p. 30

Wilkes, Roger, 'Inside Story: Kent Lodge' [www.telegraph.co.uk/finance/property/4813226/inside-story-Kent-Lodge.html]

True Crime Periodicals

Murder Casebook 40, 'Eastbourne's Doctor Death'

Murder in Mind 43 (London: Marshall Cavendish, 1998)

Real Life Crimes 1 (London: Eaglemoss Publications, 1993)

Reference Works

Anon., *Four Very Detailed Maps: London, Medieval to Modern* (London: Old House Books, 2002)

Bedford, Sybille, *The Trial of Dr Adams* (London: Simon, 1958)

Bedford, Sybille, *The Best We Can Do?* (London: Penguin, 1989)

Browne, Douglas G., *The Rise of Scotland Yard* (London: George Harrap, 1956)

Cyriax, Oliver, *The Penguin Encyclopedia of Crime* (London: Penguin, 1996)

Emsley, Clive, *The English Police: A Political and Social History* (London: Longmans, 1991)

Donaldson, William, *Rogues, Villains and Eccentrics* (London: Orion, 2004)

Gaute, J. H. H. & Odell, Robin, *The Murderers' Who's Who* (London: Pan, 1980)

Gilbert, Michael, *The Oxford Book of Legal Anecdotes* (Oxford: OUP, 1986)

Harrison, Richard, *Foul Deeds Will Rise* (London: John Long, 1958)

Hallworth, Rodney, *Where There's a Will: The Sensational Life of Dr John Bodkin Adams* (London: Capstan Press, 1983)

Home Office Report of the Departmental Committee on Detective Work and Procedure (London: HMSO, 1938)

Humphries, Travers, *Criminal Days* (London: Hodder and Stoughton, 1946)

Jackson, Robert, *The Chief: The Biography of Gordon Hewart, Lord Chief Justice of England* (London: Harrap, 1959)

Kynaston, David, *Family Britain 1951–57* (London: Bloomsbury, 2009)

Lane, Brian, *The Encyclopedia of Forensic Science* (London: Headline, 1992)

Lane, Margaret, *Edgar Wallace: The Biography of a Phenomenon* (London: Heinemann, 1939)

Lock, Joan, *Lady Policeman* (London: Michael Joseph, 1968)

Morris, Terence, and Blom-Cooper, Louis, *A Calendar of Murder: Criminal homicide in England since 1957* (London: Michael Joseph, 1964)

Morrison, A. C. L. & Hughes, Edward, *The Criminal Justice Act 1948* (London: Butterworth, 1949)

Morton, James, *East End Gangland* (London: Little, Brown, 2000)

Moss, Alan & Skinner, Keith, *The Scotland Yard Files* (London: The National Archives, 2006)

Nield, Basil, *Farewell to the Assizes* (London: Garnstone Press, 1972)

Nown, Graham, *Watching the Detectives* (London: Harper Collins, 1991)

Orwell, George, *The Collected Essays, Journalism and Letters Vol. 4* (London: Penguin, 1968)

Powell, Vincent, *The Legal Companion* (London: Robson Books, 2005)

Raine, Adrian, *The Anatomy of Violence* (London: Penguin, 2014)

Savill, Stanley, *The Police Service of England and Wales* (London: John Kempster, *Police Review*, 1913)

Scott, Sir Harold, *A Concise Encyclopedia of Crime and Criminals* (London: Andre Deutsch, 1961)

Shpayer-Makov, Haia, *The Ascent of the Detective* (Oxford: Oxford University Press, 2011)

Vandome, Nick, *Crimes and Criminals* (Edinburgh: Chambers, 1992)

Webb, Emily, *Angels of Death* (Richmond, Australia: The Five Mile Press, 2015)

Whittington-Egan, Richard, *Speaking Volumes* (Great Malvern: Cappella Archive, 2004)

Wilson, David, *A History of British Serial Killing* (London: Sphere, 2009)

Wynn, Douglas, *The Crime Writer's Handbook* (London: Allison and Busby, 2003)

Archival Sources

Note: archival sources from police records, containing letters by Bert Hannam, are in print in Pamela Cullen's book *A Stranger in Blood*. My references and quotations are therefore from Cullen's text. The archival source is at: *R v John Bodkin Adams*, Sussex Police archive, East Sussex Record Office, and *R. v John Bodkin Adams*, Metropolitan Police (Scotland Yard) archive, The National Archives. The letters in the text from Hannam's son and from his colleague are from my own archive. The quotations regarding Charles Hewett are from an unpublished reference entry written by his son, David Hewett.

The Exchange Control Act (1947) [www.unesco.org/culture/natlaws/media]
   My own manuscript collection for the reference to the nurse's diary and notebook quoted.

Internet Sources

www.biomedsearch.com
www.eastbourneherald.co.uk
www.economicshelp.org
www.lawnow.org
www.liverpoolecho.co.uk/news/liverpool-murder-most-foul-killer-sisters-3488152
www.northantstelegraph.co.uk
www.oldpolicecellsmuseum.org.uk
www.pasttimeproject.co.uk
www.terramedia.co.uk/reference/law/british

Individual essays available on the internet have also proved useful:
Normey, Rob, 'The Best We Can Do? Sybille Bedford's classic account of a famous British murder trial' [www.lawnow.org]

British Library Newspapers

'Doctors Bar Mercy Killing' *The Gloucestershire Echo* 18 October 1950 p. 1
'Doctors Reject All-In Health Plan' *Courier and Advertiser* 11 September 1950
'I Helped to End a Life' *Citizen* 26 February 1937 p. 12

'Should a Doctor Kill?' *Courier and Advertiser* 23 August 1954 p. 4

'Super-Snooping' *Courier and Advertiser* 24 September 1947 p. 2

'Notables in Too Costly Holiday Prosecution' *Daily Mail* 27 March 1947 p. 1

'Police Education' *Aberdeen Press and Journal* 12 October 1927 p. 4

'Widespread Appeal for Condemned Mother' *Western Daily Press* 3 December 1934 p. 4

'X-Ray Search for Money in Letters' *Courier and Advertiser* 24 September 1947 p. 2

'Yard Man to Probe Dollar Rackets' *The Evening Telegraph and Post* 16 August 1947 p. 3

The Times Digital Archive

'City Notes: Old Consols Under 90' 25 July 1947 p. 8

'Confidences to Doctors' 5 October 1948 p. 2

'Defeating the Criminal' 21 December 1945 p. 2

'Detectives Not Guilty of Corruption' 22 January 1944 p. 2

'Dr Adams Fined £2,400' 27 July 1957 p. 4

'Lack of Police in London' 29 September 1951

'Allegations Denied by Attorney General' 10 November 1973

'Former Detective Says He Confused Two Letters' 12 November 1973

'Trotskyist Offices in London' 6 April 1944 p. 4

'200 Detectives Wanted' 25 January 1947 p. 2

ACKNOWLEDGEMENTS

First, anyone writing on Bert Hannam owes thanks to Pamela Cullen and her indispensable book on the Adams case. Her reproduction of letters and other texts makes so much relating to Hannam's work on that investigation easily available. Much hard application to research in the same case has also been done by Jane Robins in her book on Adams.

Many people have helped with the research needed for this book. In particular I would like to thank Stuart Gibbon, ex-detective in the Metropolitan Police, and Oliver Gerrish, grandson of Molly Lefebure. Oliver kindly supplied the picture of Molly used in the book.

For essential help in researching Herbert Hannam's career, I wish to thank P. J. Aston, of the Heritage Centre of the Metropolitan Police, and Alan Lees, at NARPO House, Wakefield. Also, special thanks go to Iain Hannam, grandson of Herbert, and to David Hewett, son of DS Charles Hewett, who played such a major part in the Adams investigations. David and Iain's help and memories have been of inestimable value in the research for this book.

Correspondence with Catherine Browne and Dave (no surname) has also provided valuable sidelights on the Hannam officers. Without personal contacts and responses from appeals for memories, it would have been almost impossible to find biographical material other than in the works in print.

For initial enquiries, and the consequent help found, thanks go to the editors of *Narpo News*, the magazine for the National Association of Retired Police Officers.

For insights into the work of police detectives, thanks go again to Stuart Gibbon, former detective officer with the Metropolitan Police. An interview with Stuart was invaluable in ascertaining the nature of the Hendon training regime.

Conversations with Andy Wade, Kate Walker and with Aiden Lane were helpful also. I thank staff at the Brynmor Jones Library, University of Hull, who helped in digging out some 1950s material.

INDEX

Adams, Dr Bodkin 27–28,
    106–146
Air Ministry 50
Ashby, Dr Michael 125
Astor Club 103

Ballast Hole case (see
    Kempston) 51–57
Bermondsey 98
Bow Street Runners 38
British Medical Association 125
Brownhill, Mrs 142

Calvert, Louie 19
Camps, Dr Francis 52, 127
Canter, Ben 100
Cecil, Henry 60, 66
  *The Trial of Walter
    Rowland* 66
Christie, John 85
Clarke, Gillian 13
Cosh, PC Arthur 90

Crimes Club 19–21
Cripps, Sir Stafford 76
Crossley tenders 43
Cullen, Pamela 125–126, 179, 203

Detective magazine (France) 110
Detectives 22–23, 32–33
Devlin, Patrick 117, 123–5, 137,
    223
Dew, Walter 36
Douthwaite, Dr Arthur 125

Eastbourne 107, 232–234
Economic depression 72
Euthanasia debate 211–216
Exchange control 72–74
Exchange Control Act (1947) 76

Fahy, Sir Peter 96
Firmin, Stanley 33–34
Flying Squad 34, 44–45
Fraser, Frankie 98, 200

Freeman, William   50
Ghost Squad   34
Gibbon, Stuart   189
Goddard, Lord   64, 100
Grech, Joseph   99
Gribble, Leonard   53–56

Habitual Criminals Register   33
Hale, Leslie   66
   Hanged in Error   66
Halifax   154–167
Halifax Courier   163
Hannam, DCS Herbert
   Attacks on   30–31
   Before police career   40–41
   Character   37–38
   Childhood   40
   Financial investigations   71–82
   Record of service   8
   Rowland case   58–66
   Teddington Towpath
      case   83–94
   Training   188–189
   Wartime life   48
Hannam, Iain   182–183
Hannam, Kenneth   180–182
Hardy, Thomas   7
Hare, Sir Ronald   34
Harris, Dr   130–131
Hawkins, Mr Justice   18
Hendon (Police College)   46
Henson, Leslie   109
Hewitt, Charles   9, 37, 115,
   132–133
Hewitt, David   180, 217–228
Hitchcock, Alfred   79
Hoskins, Percy   29, 48, 57,
   184–185, 196, 202

No Hiding Place   48, 57, 188,
   195, 202
Two Men Were Acquitted   28,
   111
Hoyle, Clifford   225
Hullett, Bobbie   116, 128

Jolly, John   64–65, 68–69

Kempston (see Ballast Hole
   case)   51–52, 84
Kent Lodge (Eastbourne)   140, 233
Kimber, Billy   46
Kynaston, David   234

Lawrence, Geoffrey   117–119
Lee, Robert   34
Lefebure, Molly   51–52, 54–6,
   200
   Murder on the Home Front   57
Leicester Assizes   55
Lewes Assizes   141
Lloyd-George, David   173–174
Lyle, George   88

Macdonald, Ramsay   72
Mahar, Caitlin   213–214
Maltese immigration   99
Manchester   61–64
Manningham-Buller,
   Reginald   117
Mant, Dr Keith   88
Marston, James   171
Mass Observation   111
Mathew, *Theobald*   125
Medical Annual   129
Medical Defence Union   123–124
Miley, George   168

Mobile Patrol experiment 43
Morrell, Edith 116, 128
Morton, James 90
Moynihan, Lord Berkeley 142–146

Nixon, Inspector 199

Old Police Cells Museum 103
Omnopon (morphine
    solution) 129
Orwell, George 15, 82
Ozamis, Martin 50–51

Peel House 187, 197
Peel, Sir Robert 26
Pickering, Edward 111–112
Pierrepoint, Albert 69–70
Pilcher, Mr Justice 141
Police Review 196
Priestley, J. B. 84
Prothero, Arthur 92–93
Public Order Act (1936) 209
Pugh, DI 113
Pye, Emily 159–167, 229–231

Quincey, Thomas de 15, 25

Race course crime 44
Rawlinson, Peter 88–91
Read, Leonard 190
Ridge, Charles 103
Robins, Jane 179
Robinson, Bruce 18
    They All Love Jack 18
Roughead, William 16–18
Rowe, D.S. 162
Rowland, Walter (murder
    case) 58–66

Royal Commission on Capital
    Punishment (1953) 114
Rudkin, Inspector 86

Sabini, Charles 44–5
Savage, Percy 46
Scott, Sir Harold 98
Second World War 73–74, 97
Shawcross, Christopher 102
Shipman, Dr Harold 116, 137,
    215–216, 223
Simpson, Dr Keith 51, 53–57
'Slasher' case (Halifax) 161
Slipper, Jack 39–40
Smith, Robert 52
Snowden, Philip 72
Songhurst, Barbara 85–7
Stevenson, Melford 116
Syme, John 169–170

Tarr, Chief Inspector
    Wilfred 77–80
Teddington Lock 85
Teddy Boys 38
Thomas, Donald 128
Thoreau, Henry 15
Treasury, The 80
Trenchard, Lord 49
True crime genre 14–17
Tryhorn, Professor 162

Ware, David 62–65
Wayte, William 50
Whicher, Jonathan 35
Whiteway, Alfred 88–90
Wordsworth, William 13

Young, Commander Hugh 207